May God Bless the reader of this book!

Benjamin M. Wainwright —

This book is the property of:

_____

_____

_____

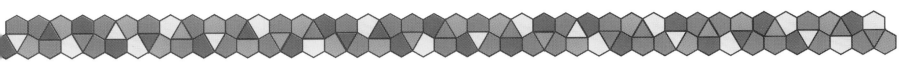

Roadside Revelations®

By Boykin Woodruff, Sr.

Revelations Publications • Mobile, Alabama

ISBN 0-9641645-0-7

Published by Revelation Publications
P.O. Box 81326
Mobile, Alabama 36608

Printed and bound in Mexico

Roadside Revelations® is a registered trademark of Boykin Woodruff, Sr.

This book is dedicated to all sign-tific theologians, whose laboratories are in the hearts of people.

In Grateful Appreciation

My thanks and grateful appreciation to my heavenly Father, who has been gracious and loving through His Son, Jesus Christ in whom I have put my trust. To my six grandchildren, who unwittingly urged Roadside Revelations® *as a publication:*

Jennifer Ann,

Sophie, III,

Kent Steven,

Abby,

Bubba,

Max, III

Preface

Welcome to "windshield theology." My windshield has been the lens to a new and exciting adventure in my daily work and travels, as I have peered through it at the signs in front of churches that I drive by. These signs, which I call *Roadside Revelations*®, have been a source of inspiration and intriguing thought. Since I had no hobbies, I wanted to compile a catalog of pictures for my grandchildren. However, as I gathered these pictures of *Roadside Revelations*®, I decided to compile this catalog for you.

This publication can become a spiritual album for the Christian. For the person who has not made the decision to become a Christian, these materials can be helpful in coming to that decision. You may find yourself in some of these pictures. Sometimes, as I took a picture of a particular message, I felt I was taking my own picture, which was not always flattering. However, these signs were a spice rack for me; they added flavor to my day. While some of the signs contain droll language, they will dwell in the mind and heart of the individual.

I was most impressed with two pictures you will find in these pages. Each left me with a compelling thought. The first one reads:

"God has two homes, one is in Heaven, one the thankful heart."

Examine yourself. Have you made God a home in your heart? Is He a homeless God due to your selfishness and disbelief? Is there room in your heart for Him? If not, why not?

After the disastrous flood in Elba, Alabama, in March of 1990, I was traveling through that community and found in front of the First Methodist Church of Elba this profound reminder:

"Elba has much to be thankful for."

This message placed in the hearts and minds of that community a spiritual levee. While you may not have to worry about a surging flood changing your lifestyle, you do need the levee of gratitude. Being thankful should be a spiritual component of our lives.

All of us should be more grateful for the blessings of God in our lives. We should be thankful for God's gift of eternal life through Jesus Christ, His Son. We should be thankful for the freedom we enjoy in this great country.

If you do not know Christ, and this book has been a help in your making a decision, visit the church of your choice, inform the minister you are from the "Roadside," and you will be given proper instructions and direction to help you reach your destination. The Holy Bible will be your best road map!

B. Woodruff, Sr.

FIRST BAPTIST CHURCH
OF DEARMANVILLE

CARS ARE NOT
THE ONLY THING
RECALLED BY THEIR
MAKER

Celeste Road
Church of God
PASTOR: MUSIC:

MEN ARE WHAT THEIR
MOTHERS MAKE THEM

BEATLINE
BAPTIST CHURCH
FOR INWARD PEACE
TRY THE
UPWARD LOOK

Moffat Road
Assembly of God

THE MAN WHO
KNEELS TO GOD
CAN STAND UP
TO ANYTHING

MANS LOVE HAS LIMITS
GODS LOVE IS LIMITLESS

WELCOME
First Assembly of God
THERE WILL BE
NO
FIRE ESCAPE
IN HELL
REV. KENNETH MORRIS: PASTOR

SUN. SCHOOL 9:45 A.M.
WORSHIP 10:45 A.M.
SUN. EVE. 6:00 P.M.
WED. 7:00 P.M.

Assembly of God
"GOD USES
OAK TREES,
NOT
MUSHROOMS"

DELAY IS
NOT DENIAL -
PRAY ON!

THE CHRISTIAN WHO
ROWS THE CHURCH
BOAT DOESN'T HAVE
TIME TO ROCK IT !

WHEN YOU CAN'T TRACE THE HAND
OF GOD, YOU CAN TRUST HIS HEART.
SUNDAY SCHOOL 9:45AM   WORSHIP 11:00 AM 6:00PM   WED EVE 7:00 PM
PASTOR : GLENN VAUGHN

GOD'S WORD NEVER CHANGES BUT IT CHANGES THINGS

SEVEN HILLS
BAPTIST CHURCH

*THE HARVEST IS
PLENTIFUL, BUT THE
LABORERS ARE FEW !
HAVE YOU REAPED
YOUR SHARE ?

OAK GROVE MISSIONARY BAPTIST CHURCH

IT'S EXTREMELY DIFFICULT FOR A CHILD TO LIVE RIGHT IF HE HAS NEVER SEEN IT DONE

PRAYERLESS PEWS MAKE POWERLESS PULPITS

COURAGE IS FEAR THAT HAS SAID ITS PRAYERS

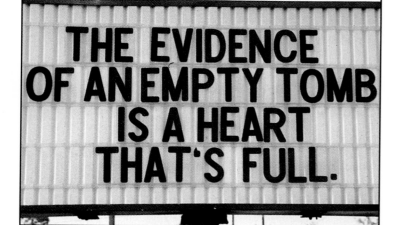

THE EVIDENCE OF AN EMPTY TOMB IS A HEART THAT'S FULL.

HERITAGE BAPTIST CHURCH
OF PENSACOLA

SUNDAY SCHOOL 9:30AM — WORSHIP 10:00AM & 6:00PM — WED. 7:00PM — JERALD L. MANLEY Pastor

NO ONE IS RICH ENOUGH
TO BUY BACK THE PAST

FOUR MILE CREEK
BAPTIST CHURCH

THE WAGES OF SIN
HAVE NEVER BEEN
REDUCED

AMBASSADOR
BAPTIST CHURCH

SUN 10 AM
SUN 6 PM
WED 7 PM

GOD WITHOUT MAN IS
STILL GOD/MAN WITHOUT
GOD IS STILL WITHOUT!

First Baptist Church
of Kushla

EDSON DREW PASTOR

THOSE WHO WALK WITH GOD
ALWAYS REACH THEIR
DESTINATION

WORSHIP 11:00am & 7:00pm — SUNDAY SCHOOL 9:45am — CHURCH TRAINING 6:00pm — PRAYER Wed. 7:00pm

SPRING HILL
BAPTIST CHURCH

OCTOBER 31
NO TRICKS . . . JUST TREATS!
WORSHIP WITH US SUNDAY
BIBLE STUDY 9:30AM WORSHIP 10:45AM

A HUG
ONE SIZE FITS ALL

Church of Christ

SUNDAY	GET EVEN
930	WITH THE ONES
1030	THAT HAVE DONE
600	THE MOST FOR YOU
WED	
700	

YOUR CHILDREN
NEED YOUR
PRESENCE
MORE THAN
YOUR PRESENTS

Moffat Road Assembly of God

WHAT WE DO REVEALS MORE THAN WHAT WE CLAIM TO BELIEVE

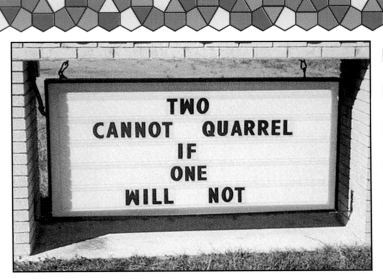

TWO CANNOT QUARREL IF ONE WILL NOT

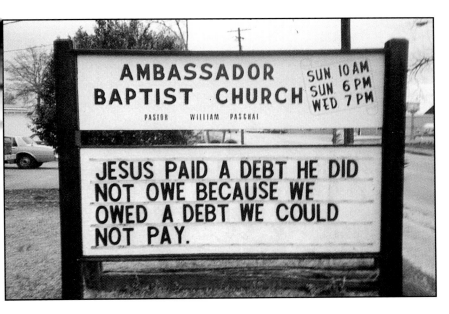

AMBASSADOR BAPTIST CHURCH
SUN 10 AM
SUN 6 PM
WED 7 PM
PASTOR WILLIAM PASCHAL

JESUS PAID A DEBT HE DID NOT OWE BECAUSE WE OWED A DEBT WE COULD NOT PAY.

SOUTHERN BAPTIST
FIRST BAPTIST CHURCH
SUNDAY SCHOOL 9:45 A.M.   SUNDAY WORSHIP   CHURCH TRAINING 5:45 P.M.   WEDNESDAY PRAYER MEETING

THE GREATEST FREEDOM FREEDOM FROM SIN

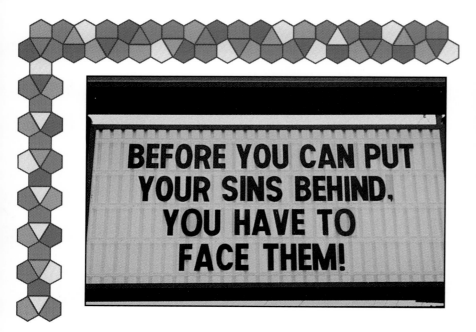

BEFORE YOU CAN PUT YOUR SINS BEHIND, YOU HAVE TO FACE THEM!

Gulfcrest Baptist Church
ETERNAL LIFE COMES BY TRUSTING JESUS

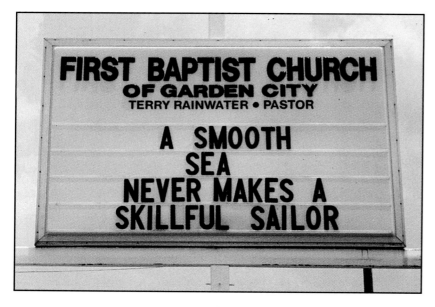

FIRST BAPTIST CHURCH
OF GARDEN CITY
TERRY RAINWATER • PASTOR

A SMOOTH SEA NEVER MAKES A SKILLFUL SAILOR

WHEN LOVE AND SKILL WORK TOGETHER EXPECT A MASTERPIECE

WESTERN HILLS
Church of Christ
A FOOL AND
H S MONEY
ARE SOON
SPOTTED

FIRST BAPTIST CHURCH
of
HILLSBORO

WHEN A CHURCH
STOPS DOING
IT STARTS
DYING

SUNDAY SCHOOL 9:45   WORSHIP 11:00
TONY BILLIONS, PASTOR

NEW HOPE
ASSEMBLY OF GOD
DYKES L. STRICKLING · PASTOR

HELL AND DESTRUCTION
ARE NEVER FULL. THE EYES
OF MAN ARE NEVER
SATISFIED PRO. 27:20

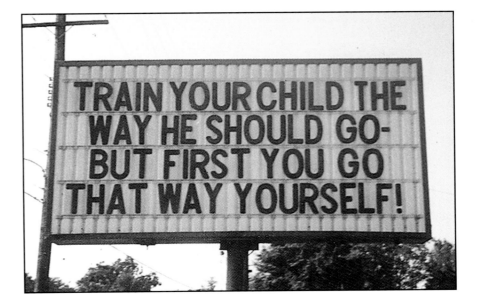

TRAIN YOUR CHILD THE
WAY HE SHOULD GO-
BUT FIRST YOU GO
THAT WAY YOURSELF!

JESUS IS THE LIGHT IN A LOST & DYING WORLD

AMBASSADOR BAPTIST CHURCH

SUN. 10 AM
SUN. 6 PM
WED. 7 PM

PASTOR WILLIAM PASCHAL

MOREOVER IT IS REQUIRED IN STEWARDS. THAT A MAN BE FOUND FAITHFUL.

I COR. 4:2

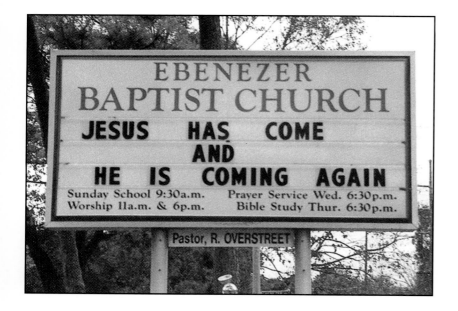

EBENEZER BAPTIST CHURCH

JESUS HAS COME AND HE IS COMING AGAIN

Sunday School 9:30a.m.   Prayer Service Wed. 6:30p.m.
Worship 11a.m. & 6p.m.   Bible Study Thur. 6:30p.m.

Pastor, R. OVERSTREET

OXFORD CHURCH of CHRIST

THE LORD ALSO

HELPS THOSE WHO

HELP OTHERS

WESTERN HILLS
Church of Christ

THE RESULT OF A
WALK WITH GOD IS
WORK FOR GOD

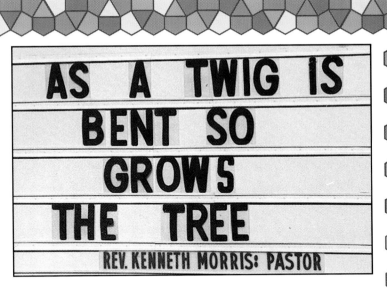

AS A TWIG IS
BENT SO
GROWS
THE TREE
REV. KENNETH MORRIS: PASTOR

Gulfcrest Baptist Church
ENTER TO WORSHIP
DEPART
TO SERVE

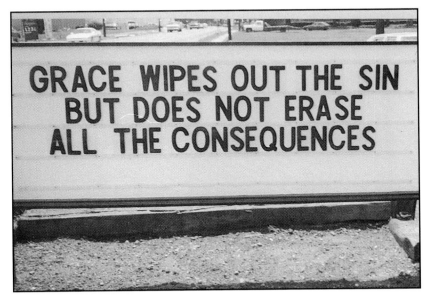

GRACE WIPES OUT THE SIN
BUT DOES NOT ERASE
ALL THE CONSEQUENCES

Old Spanish Fort
BAPTIST CHURCH
→ NEXT RIGHT →
GOD WILL NEVER GUIDE
WHERE HE
DOES NOT PROVIDE
WORSHIP 830 1100 630
7100

THE
GREATER ANTIOCH
MISSIONARY BAPTIST
CHURCH
DR. JOHN W. DAVIS, SR. — PASTOR
PROBLEMS ARE
GUIDELINES,
NOT STOP
SIGNS

A CHRISTAIN
IS A LIVING SERMON
WHETHER OR NOT HE
PREACH A WORD

THE BEST THING
TO SPEND ON
YOUR CHILDREN
IS YOUR TIME.

NO REWARDS
ARE OFFERED
FOR FINDING
FAULTS.

Rev. J.H. WILLIAMS
PASTOR

SOME CHURCHES
ARE SOUND IN DOCTRINE,
BUT THEY ARE ALSO
SOUND ASLEEP

BRENTWOOD
ASSEMBLY OF GOD

GOD NEVER
TURNS OFF HIS
SECURITY SYSTEM

ONE WHO TRIES TO
BUY HIS WAY INTO
HEAVEN WILL GET
SOLD OUT

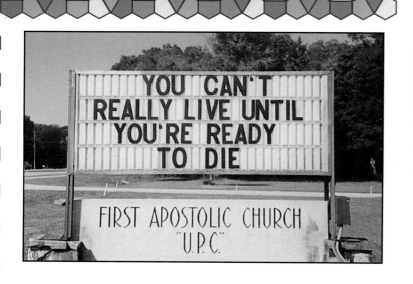

YOU CAN'T REALLY LIVE UNTIL YOU'RE READY TO DIE

FIRST APOSTOLIC CHURCH "U.P.C."

First Baptist Church of Kushla

EDSON DREW PASTOR

ONE THING YOU CAN GIVE AND STILL KEEP IS YOUR WORD

WORSHIP	SUNDAY SCHOOL	CHURCH TRAINING	PRAYER
11:00am & 7:00pm	9:45am	6:00pm	Wed. 7:00pm

First Baptist Church
Windsor Park

Sunday School 10 am • Worship Service 11 am
Sunday Evening 6 pm • Wednesday Evening 7pm

IF YOUR LIFE IS ON EMPTY, TURN IN FOR A FILL UP

LAKEVIEW BAPTIST CHURCH

NEVER TAKE A VACATION FROM GOD

Celeste Road
Church of God
PASTOR: MUSIC:

BIBLE
BASIC INSTRUCTIONS
BEFORE LEAVING
EARTH

INDEPENDENT   FUNDAMENTAL

BELLINGRATH ROAD
BAPTIST CHURCH

SUNDAY SCHOOL   10:00 AM
MORNING WORSHIP   10:30 AM
EVENING WORSHIP   6:00 PM
WED BIBLE STUDY   7:00 PM

PASTOR DR ARVEL BROCKWELL
VISITORS WELCOME   PH 973-1465

FAITHFULNESS IN LITTLE
THINGS IS A GREAT
THING

WELCOME

WAYNE COUNTY
BAPTIST
ASSOCIATION

PEOPLE WILL BELIEVE
ANYTHING IF YOU
WHISPER IT

TRY GOD:
IF YOU DON'T LIKE
HIM THE DEVIL WILL
TAKE YOU BACK!

WHEN YOU ARE AT THE
END OF YOUR ROPE
TIE A KNOT AND
HOLD ON

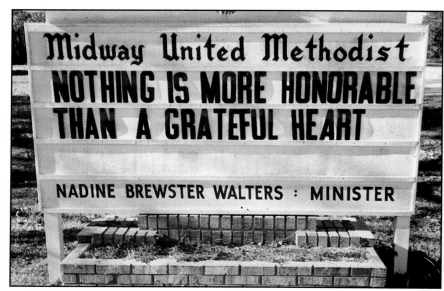

Midway United Methodist
NOTHING IS MORE HONORABLE
THAN A GRATEFUL HEART

NADINE BREWSTER WALTERS : MINISTER

ZION BAPTIST CHURCH

THE ORNAMENTS OF
A HOUSE ARE THE
FRIENDS WHO VISIT IT
REV. KENNETH FARLEY

Gulfcrest Baptist Church
THE BIBLE LIGHTS THE
PATHWAY TO HEAVEN

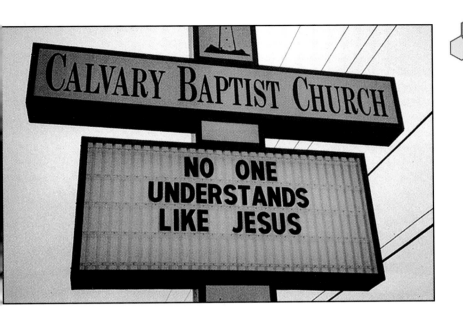

CALVARY BAPTIST CHURCH

NO ONE
UNDERSTANDS
LIKE JESUS

GOOD WITHOUT
GOD BECOMES
★ O. ★

EAST MOSS POINT
BAPTIST CHURCH

S/S 9:45AM   WORSHIP 11:00AM 6:00PM   C/T 5:00PM   WED. 7:00PM

GOD'S GIFT TO A DYING WORLD
IS THE LIFE-GIVING SAVIOR.

DR. HAROLD ANDERSON, PASTOR

SUN. 10 AM
SUN. 6 PM
WED. 7 PM

AMBASSADOR
BAPTIST CHURCH

PASTOR   WILLIAM PASCHAL

EVERY SINNER MUST
BE PARDONED OR
PUNISHED

THE
GREATER ANTIOCH
MISSIONARY BAPTIST
CHURCH
DR. JOHN W DAVIS SR — PASTOR

WE FIND A JOY IN
LIVING BY THE
KINDNESS WE SHOW
TO OTHERS

MOVELLA
ASSEMBLY OF GOD

A FIRE KINDLED AGAINST
AN ENEMY OFTEN BURNS
YOU MORE THAN HIM

HOW LONG SINCE
YOU KNEELED
AT THE CROSS?

SAGE AVENUE
UNITED
METHODIST CHURCH

WILL YOU MAKE ROOM
IN YOUR INN
FOR JESUS
IN 1994?

Service Hours
Sunday 11:00 AM & 6:00 PM
Sunday School 9:45 AM
Rev. Howard Bozeman, Pastor

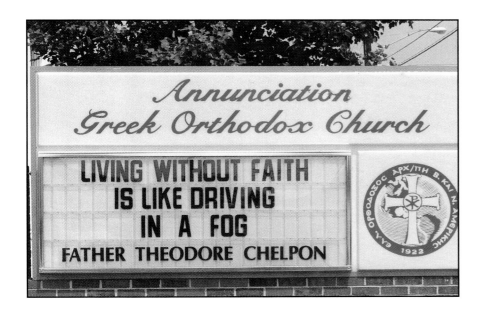

Annunciation
Greek Orthodox Church

LIVING WITHOUT FAITH
IS LIKE DRIVING
IN A FOG
FATHER THEODORE CHELPON

FIRST PENTECOSTAL
CHURCH
ACTS 2:38
HOME OF
THE OLD TIME RELIGION

ITS NOT
IMPORTANT WHO
YOU ARE BUT
WHOSE YOU ARE!

WEEKLY SERVICES
SUNDAY MORNING 10AM ~ EVENING 6PM
WEDNESDAY BIBLE STUDY 7 PM

Old Spanish Fort
BAPTIST CHURCH
← NEXT LEFT →
PROSPERITY
ATTRACTS FRIENDS
ADVERSITY
TELLS YOU WHO THEY ARE

IT'S A CHILD
NOT A CHOICE

BEATLINE
BAPTIST CHURCH
CHRIST IN THE HEART
IS
HEAVEN ON EARTH

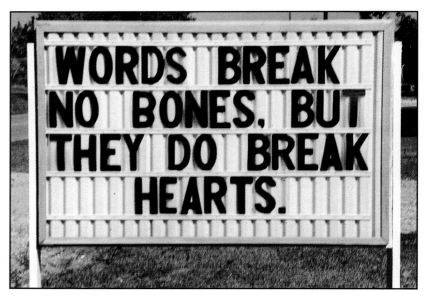

WORDS BREAK
NO BONES, BUT
THEY DO BREAK
HEARTS.

THE WEATHER
N E V E R
CHANGES
IN HELL !

MAKE NEW FRIENDS
BUT KEEP THE OLD
ONE IS LIKE SILVER
THE OTHER IS GOLD

AMBASSADOR BAPTIST CHURCH
SUN 10 AM
SUN 6 PM
WED 7 PM

WHEN TROUBLE KNOCKS SEND JESUS TO THE DOOR!

MEN DO NOT FAIL THEY GIVE UP TRYING

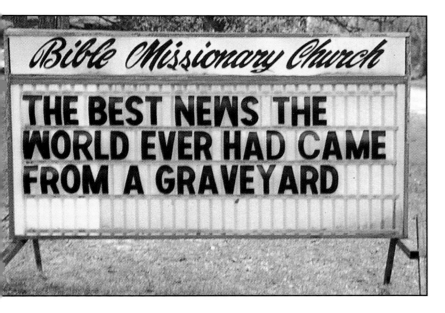

Bible Missionary Church

THE BEST NEWS THE WORLD EVER HAD CAME FROM A GRAVEYARD

IF YOU HAVE A GOOD EXCUSE. DON'T USE IT.

BELLINGRATH ROAD BAPTIST CHURCH

SUNDAY SCHOOL 10:00 AM
MORNING WORSHIP 10:30 AM
EVENING WORSHIP 6:00 PM
WED. BIBLE STUDY 7:00 PM

PASTOR DR ARVEL BROCKWELL
VISITORS WELCOME   PH. 973-1465

YOU CAN NEVER
BURY YOUR INFLUENCE

WELCOME

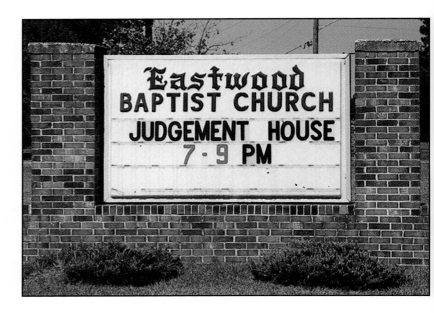

Eastwood BAPTIST CHURCH
JUDGEMENT HOUSE
7-9 PM

Church of Christ

SUNDAY IF I GET ON MY KNEES
930
1030   GOD HELPS ME STAND UP
600
WED   TO   ANYTHNIG
700

SAGE AVENUE
UNITED
METHODIST CHURCH

IF YOU'RE STANDING
ON GOD'S PROMISES
YOU WILL NOT FALL
FOR 'SATAN' LIES!

Service Hours
Sunday 11:00 AM & 7:00 PM
Sunday School 9:45 AM
Rev. Howard Bozeman, Pastor

oak park church of God

DO LESS FOR JR.
AND MORE
WITH HIM

SUNDAY SCHOOL 10 AM
MORNING WORSHIP
10:45
PRAISE GATHERING
6:30 PM

DR. SAM LUKE, PASTOR

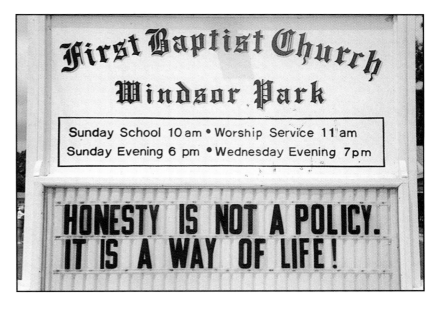

First Baptist Church
Windsor Park

Sunday School 10 am • Worship Service 11 am
Sunday Evening 6 pm • Wednesday Evening 7 pm

HONESTY IS NOT A POLICY.
IT IS A WAY OF LIFE!

THE CROWNS
WE WEAR IN HEAVEN
MUST BE
WON ON EARTH

GOD
WORKS
HERE

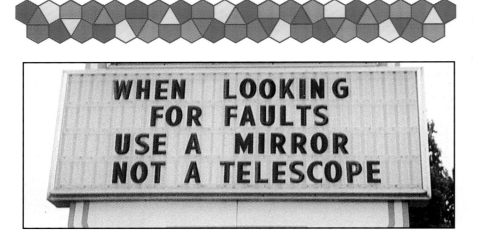

WHEN LOOKING
FOR FAULTS
USE A MIRROR
NOT A TELESCOPE

BEHOLD THE LORDS
HAND IS NOT
SHORTENED THAT
IT CANNOT SAVE...
READ ISA. 59

First Baptist Church
Windsor Park

Sunday School 10 am • Worship Service 11 am
Sunday Evening 6 pm • Wednesday Evening 7 pm

NO JESUS NO PEACE!
BUT IF YOU
KNOW JESUS KNOW PEACE!

Gulfcrest Baptist Church

BE A REFLECTOR LET
JESUS BE SEEN IN YOU

WELCOME

First Assembly of God

PRAY
BELIEVE - RECIEVE
PRAY
DOUBT - DO WITHOUT

SUN. SCHOOL 9:45 A.M.
WORSHIP 10:45 A.M.
SUN. EVE. 6:00 P.M.
WED. 7:00 P.M.

REV. KENNETH MORRIS: PASTOR

EVERYTHING COMES
TO HIM WHO WAITS.
IF HE WORKS WHILE
HE WAITS

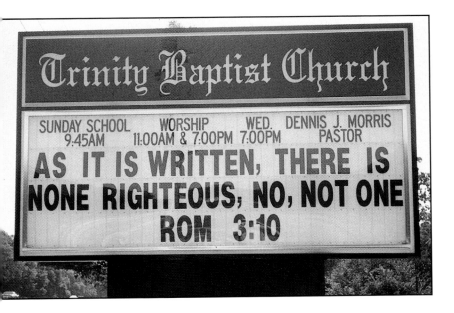

Trinity Baptist Church

SUNDAY SCHOOL 9:45AM WORSHIP 11:00AM & 7:00PM WED. 7:00PM DENNIS J. MORRIS PASTOR

AS IT IS WRITTEN, THERE IS
NONE RIGHTEOUS, NO, NOT ONE
ROM 3:10

AMBASSADOR
BAPTIST CHURCH
PASTOR WILLIAM PASCHAL

SUN. 10 AM
SUN. 6 PM
WED. 7 PM

YOU CAN SERVE WITHOUT
LOVING BUT YOU CANNOT
LOVE WITHOUT SERVING.

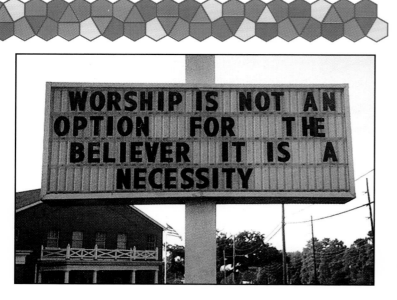

WORSHIP IS NOT AN OPTION FOR THE BELIEVER IT IS A NECESSITY

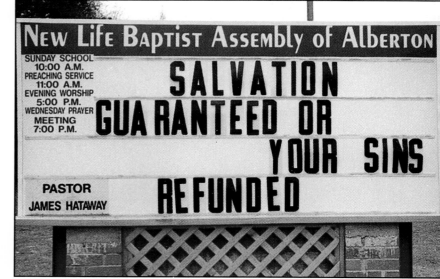

New Life Baptist Assembly of Alberton

SUNDAY SCHOOL
10:00 A.M.
PREACHING SERVICE
11:00 A.M.
EVENING WORSHIP
5:00 P.M.
WEDNESDAY PRAYER
MEETING
7:00 P.M.

PASTOR
JAMES HATAWAY

SALVATION GUARANTEED OR YOUR SINS REFUNDED

First Baptist Church
St. Stephens

SIN BLINDS OUR EYES
GRACE OPENS THEM

PASTOR HENRY McDUFFIE

THE CHRISTIANS LIFE IS THE WORLDS BIBLE

WE DO WRONG WHEN
WE FAIL TO DO RIGHT

First Baptist
Church
Rev. J.H. WILLIAMS
PASTOR

PRAYER MUST MEAN
SOMETHING TO US
IF IT IS TO MEAN
ANYTHING TO GOD

IS HE LORD OF
ALL, OR
NOT AT ALL?

MOVELLA
ASSEMBLY OF GOD

JUDGE YOURSELF BEFORE
YOU JUDGE OTHERS

BIBLE BAPTIST CHURCH

HEAVEN FOR THE CHRISTIAN IS BEST SPELLED H O M E

LOST TIME IS NEVER FOUND

RON MURPHY   PASTOR

Pace Assembly of God

THE HARVEST IS GREAT... JOIN US AS WE GATHER IT IN!

FIRST ASSEMBLY OF GOD

WHEN SATAN BEGINS PREYING CHRISTIANS ARE PRAYING

Moffat Road
Assembly of God

WITH FAITH
YOU DON'T HAVE
TO SEE IT
TO BELIEVE IT

WESTERN HILLS
Church of Christ

YOU CANNOT
STAND UP
TO WASH FEET

First Baptist Church
of Kushla

EDSON DREW PASTOR

ALL SERVICE RANKS THE
SAME WITH GOD   THERE IS
NO LAST NOR FIRST

WORSHIP   SUNDAY SCHOOL   CHURCH TRAINING   PRAYER
11:00am & 7:00pm   9:45am   6:00pm   Wed. 7:00pm

THERE ARE
TOO MANY
SEMI-CHRISTIANS

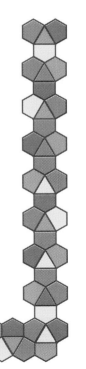

NEED A FAITH LIFT!
COME TO
GODS
HOUSE

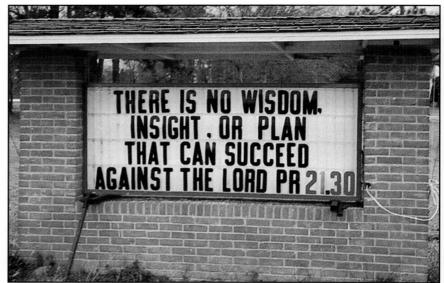

THERE IS NO WISDOM.
INSIGHT. OR PLAN
THAT CAN SUCCEED
AGAINST THE LORD PR 21.30

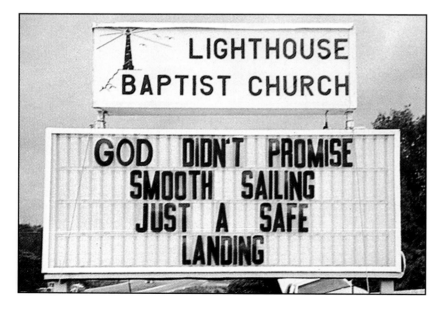

LIGHTHOUSE
BAPTIST CHURCH

GOD DIDN'T PROMISE
SMOOTH SAILING
JUST A SAFE
LANDING

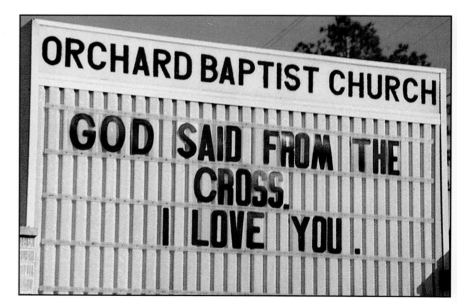

ORCHARD BAPTIST CHURCH

GOD SAID FROM THE
CROSS.
I LOVE YOU.

SOME PEOPLE NEVER GET INTERESTED IN A THING UNTIL IT IS NONE OF THEIR BUSINESS

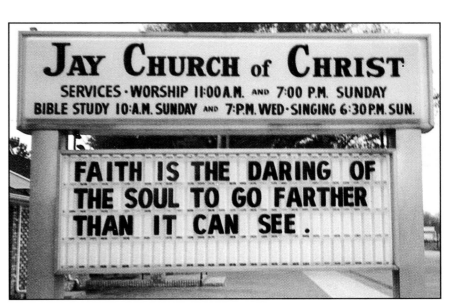

JAY CHURCH of CHRIST

SERVICES · WORSHIP 11:00 A.M. AND 7:00 P.M. SUNDAY
BIBLE STUDY 10 A.M. SUNDAY AND 7 P.M. WED · SINGING 6:30 P.M. SUN.

FAITH IS THE DARING OF THE SOUL TO GO FARTHER THAN IT CAN SEE.

First Baptist Church of Kushla

EDSON DREW PASTOR

YOU CAN BUY EDUCATION BUT WISDOM IS A GIFT OF GOD

WORSHIP 11:00am & 7:00pm SUNDAY SCHOOL 9:45am CHURCH TRAINING 6:00pm PRAYER Wed. 7:00pm

AMBASSADOR BAPTIST CHURCH
PASTOR: WILLIAM PASCHAL
SUN. 10:00 AM
SUN. 6:00 PM
WED. 7:00 PM

GOD'S BIGGEST PROBLEM WITH WORKERS IN HIS VINEYARD IS ABSENTEEISM

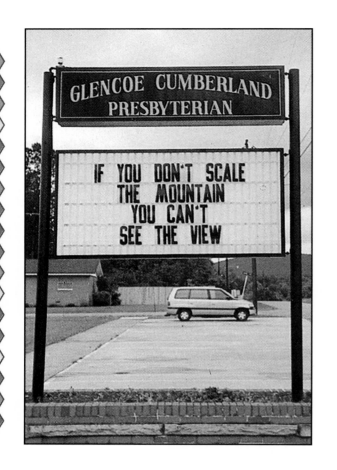

GLENCOE CUMBERLAND PRESBYTERIAN

IF YOU DON'T SCALE
THE MOUNTAIN
YOU CAN'T
SEE THE VIEW

Gulfcrest Baptist Church

A BIBLE VERSE A DAY
HELPS KEEP THE DEVIL
AWAY

AMBASSADOR
BAPTIST CHURCH

SUN. 10 AM
SUN. 6 PM
WED. 7 PM

PASTOR WILLIAM PASCHAL

GOD NEVER GIVES US HIS
WILL TO CONSIDER.

HEAVEN'S
A
PRAYER
AWAY...

Bible Missionary Church

YOU CANT BRIBE GODS GRAND JURY WHEN YOU COME TO JUDGEMENT

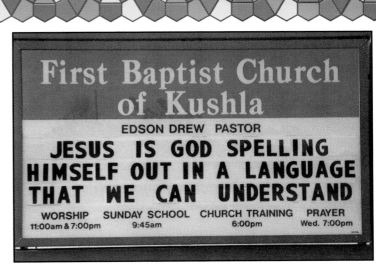

First Baptist Church of Kushla

EDSON DREW PASTOR

JESUS IS GOD SPELLING HIMSELF OUT IN A LANGUAGE THAT WE CAN UNDERSTAND

WORSHIP	SUNDAY SCHOOL	CHURCH TRAINING	PRAYER
11:00am & 7:00pm	9:45am	6:00pm	Wed. 7:00pm

EAST MOSS POINT BAPTIST CHURCH

S/S 9:45AM WORSHIP 11:00AM 6:00PM C/T 5:00PM WED. 7:00PM

GIVE UP WHAT GRIEVES THE LORD.

DR. HAROLD ANDERSON, PASTOR

FIRST BAPTIST CHURCH
— STATE LINE, MS. —

THE LOVE WE GIVE IS THE ONLY LOVE WE KEEP

S.S. 10-00 AM   D.T. 6-00 PM

GOD'S WORD
WILL NEVER FAIL.
READ IT TODAY!

PASTOR, RICK VINSON

A SUCCESSFUL MAN GETS
UP ONE TIME MORE THAN
HE'S KNOCKED DOWN

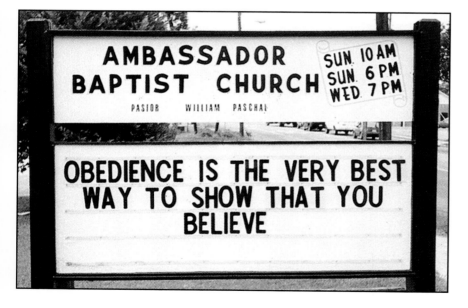

AMBASSADOR
BAPTIST CHURCH
PASTOR WILLIAM PASCHAL

SUN. 10 AM
SUN. 6 PM
WED. 7 PM

OBEDIENCE IS THE VERY BEST
WAY TO SHOW THAT YOU
BELIEVE

WESTERN HILLS
Church of Christ

NO ONE ELSE BUT
YOU CAN DO EXACTLY
WHAT YOU DO

The Christian LIGHTHOUSE
• PASTOR: TERRY HOSMER •

Sunday School 10ᴬᴹ | Sunday Evening 6ᴾᴹ
Sunday Worship 11ᴬᴹ | Wednesday Evening 7ᴾᴹ

LOVE MAKES ALL HARD HEARTS GENTLE

IT IS MORE IMPORTANT TO WATCH HOW A MAN LIVES THAN TO LISTEN TO WHAT HE SAID

FIRST BAPTIST CHURCH
PASTOR: Dr. Adrian J. Pater

THE WORD, NOT THE WORLD IS OUR STANDARD.

GOD'S MERCY IS GREATER THAN OUR MISTAKES.

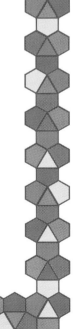

A WAYWARD CHILD IS SOMETIMES STRAIGHTENED OUT BY BEING BENT OVER

FIRST BAPTIST CHURCH
OF GARDEN CITY
• PASTOR

NOTHING WITH GOD IS ACCIDENTAL

WHAT WE DO REVEALS MORE THAN WHAT WE CLAIM TO BELIEVE

Old Spanish Fort BAPTIST CHURCH
◄ NEXT LEFT ►
A FREE TRIP TO HEAVEN DETAILS INSIDE

7100

THE DARKEST HOUR HAS BUT 60 MINUTES

Celeste Road Church of God
PASTOR: Music:

THE ROAD TO HELL IS PAVED WITH GOOD INTENTIONS.

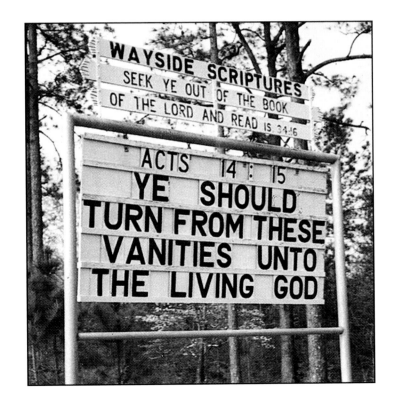

WAYSIDE SCRIPTURES
SEEK YE OUT OF THE BOOK OF THE LORD AND READ is 34:16

ACTS 14:15
YE SHOULD TURN FROM THESE VANITIES UNTO THE LIVING GOD

Bible Missionary Church

TO CHANGE EVERYTHING SIMPLY CHANGE YOUR ATTITUDE

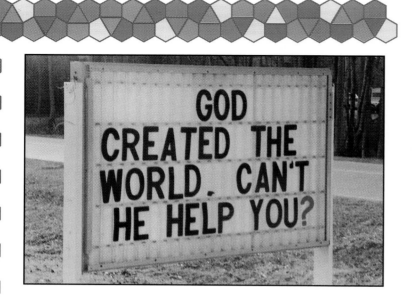

GOD CREATED THE WORLD. CAN'T HE HELP YOU?

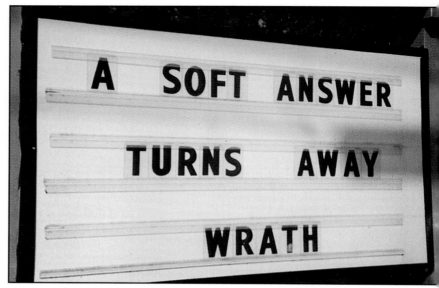

A SOFT ANSWER TURNS AWAY WRATH

First Baptist Church of Kushla

EDSON DREW PASTOR

PEOPLE ALL OVER THE WORLD SMILE IN THE SAME LANGUAGE

WORSHIP 11:00am & 7:00pm   SUNDAY SCHOOL 9:45am   CHURCH TRAINING 6:00pm   PRAYER Wed. 7:00pm

HIGHLAND CHURCH OF CHRIST

DOES YOUR WALLET HAVE HOLES? HAG 1:2-15

WELCOME
First Assembly of God

WHERE WILL
YOU SPEND
ETERNITY!

SUN. SCHOOL 9:45 A.M.
WORSHIP 10:45 A.M.
SUN. EVE. 6:00 P.M.
WED. 7:00 P.M.

REV. KENNETH MORRIS: PASTOR

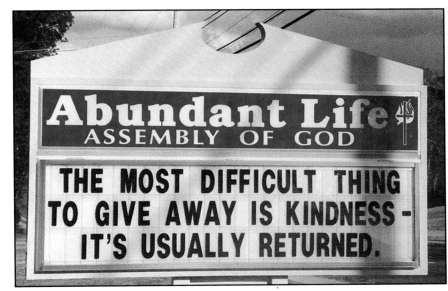

Abundant Life
ASSEMBLY OF GOD

THE MOST DIFFICULT THING
TO GIVE AWAY IS KINDNESS —
IT'S USUALLY RETURNED.

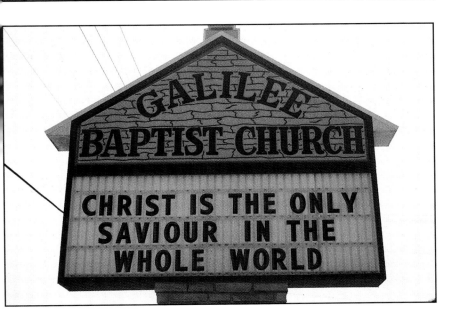

GALILEE
BAPTIST CHURCH

CHRIST IS THE ONLY
SAVIOUR IN THE
WHOLE WORLD

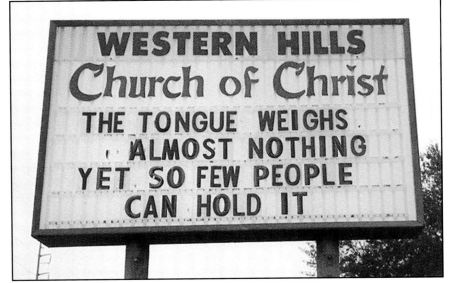

WESTERN HILLS
Church of Christ

THE TONGUE WEIGHS
ALMOST NOTHING
YET SO FEW PEOPLE
CAN HOLD IT

A PLACE TO
CALL HOME
BRING YOUR
FAMILY

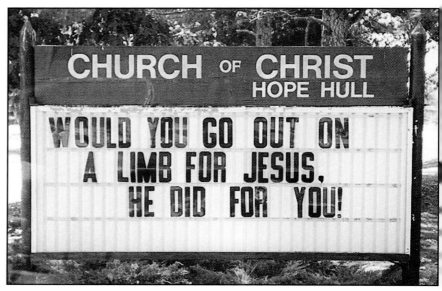

CHURCH OF CHRIST
HOPE HULL

WOULD YOU GO OUT ON
A LIMB FOR JESUS,
HE DID FOR YOU!

WESTERN HILLS
Church of Christ
JESUS NEVER SAID IT
WOULD B EEASY
HE SAID IT WOULD
B E WORTH IT

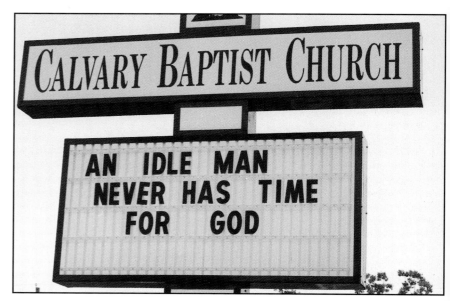

CALVARY BAPTIST CHURCH

AN IDLE MAN
NEVER HAS TIME
FOR GOD

BETTER TO BITE
YOUR TONGUE
THAN LET IT
BITE SOMEONE ELSE

Bay Vista
Baptist Church

THE EYES
OF THE
LORD
ARE
EVERYWHERE

FIRST BAPTIST CHURCH

WE BELIEVE IN
OUTREACH FOR
THE UNREACHED

PASTOR ED HEPTINSTALL

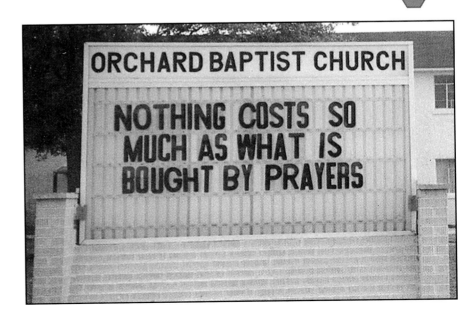

ORCHARD BAPTIST CHURCH

NOTHING COSTS SO
MUCH AS WHAT IS
BOUGHT BY PRAYERS

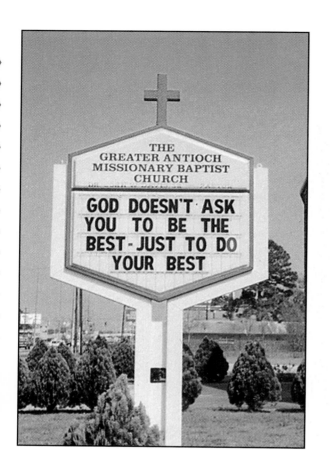

THE
GREATER ANTIOCH
MISSIONARY BAPTIST
CHURCH

GOD DOESN'T ASK
YOU TO BE THE
BEST - JUST TO DO
YOUR BEST

GALILEE
BAPTIST CHURCH

REPENTANCE TOWARD
GOD IS NECESSARY
PENANCE IS NOT

A BAD HABIT IS LIKE A
COMFORTABLE BED -
EASY TO GET INTO BUT
HARD TO GET OUT OF

THERE ARE MANY ROADS
TO HELL
BUT

JESUS IS THE ONLY PATH
TO HEAVEN

AMBASSADOR BAPTIST CHURCH
SUN 10 AM
SUN 6 PM
WED 7 PM
PASTOR WILLIAM PASCHAL

I LOVE THEM THAT LOVE ME:
AND THOSE THAT SEEK ME
EARLY SHALL FIND ME.
PROV 8:17

WE MAY NOT HAVE
ALL WE DESIRE
BUT THANK GOD
WE DONT HAVE
ALL WE DESERVE

IF OPPORTUNITY
DOES NOT KNOCK
BUILD A DOOR

First Baptist Church
of Kushla
EDSON DREW PASTOR
THOSE WHO WALK WITH GOD
ALWAYS REACH THEIR
DESTINATION
WORSHIP   SUNDAY SCHOOL   CHURCH TRAINING   PRAYER
11:00am & 7:00pm   9:45am   6:00pm   Wed. 7:00pm

JASPER CHURCH OF THE NAZARENE

MAN'S UNBELIEF DOES NOT MAKE GOD A LIAR!

SAGE AVENUE UNITED METHODIST CHURCH

THE CROSS - GOD'S CHRISTMAS GIFT FOR THE WORLD!

Service Hours
Sunday 11:00 AM & 6:00 PM
Sunday School 9:45 AM
Rev. Howard Bozeman, Pastor

Christian Fellowship TABERNACLE

THOSE WHO FOLLOW THE CROWD SOON GET LOST IN THE CROWD!

Pathway Temple

PASTOR HENRY McDUFFIE
ACT FAITH AND IT WILL BRING RESULTS

First Church of the Nazarene

THE EXPERT IN ANYTHING

WAS ONCE A BEGINNER

BE A SON WORSHIPPER.
NOT A SUN WORSHIPPER

IT'S NOT THE MOON
WE NEED TO REACH
BUT GOD WHO
PUT IT THERE

WESTERN HILLS
Church of Christ
YOU CANNOT
IMPROVE UPON
DOING THINGS
GOD'S WAY

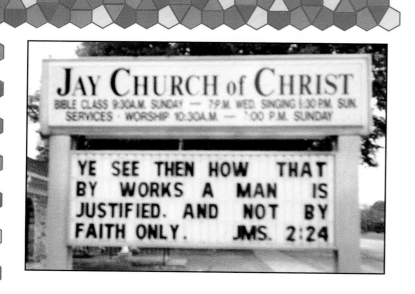

JAY CHURCH of CHRIST
BIBLE CLASS 9:30 A.M. SUNDAY — 7 P.M. WED. SINGING 1:30 P.M. SUN.
SERVICES - WORSHIP 10:30 A.M. — 7:00 P.M. SUNDAY

YE SEE THEN HOW THAT BY WORKS A MAN IS JUSTIFIED. AND NOT BY FAITH ONLY. JMS. 2:24

First Baptist Church of Kushla
EDSON DREW PASTOR
FOLKS WITH A LOT OF BRASS ARE SELDOM POLISHED
WORSHIP 11:00am & 7:00pm SUNDAY SCHOOL 9:45am CHURCH TRAINING 6:00pm PRAYER Wed. 7:00pm

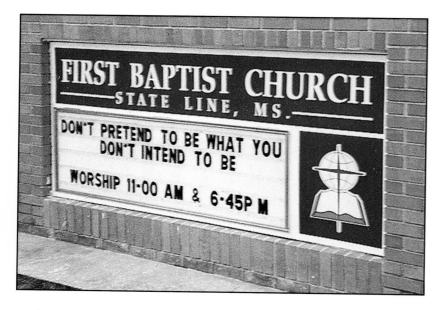

FIRST BAPTIST CHURCH
STATE LINE, MS.
DON'T PRETEND TO BE WHAT YOU DON'T INTEND TO BE
WORSHIP 11:00 AM & 6:45 PM

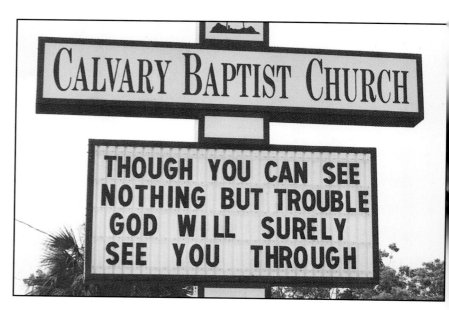

CALVARY BAPTIST CHURCH
THOUGH YOU CAN SEE NOTHING BUT TROUBLE GOD WILL SURELY SEE YOU THROUGH

Celeste Road Church of God

PASTOR: MUSIC:

CHRISTIANITY SHOULD BE A STEERING WHEEL NOT A SPARE TIRE

IN PRAYER IT IS BETTER TO HAVE A HEART WITHOUT WORDS THAN WORDS WITHOUT A HEART.

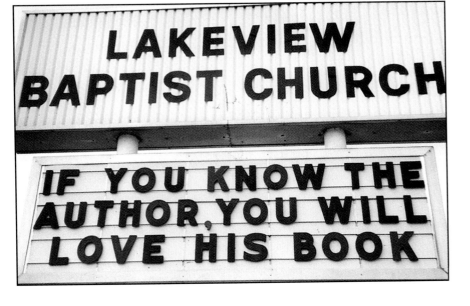

LAKEVIEW BAPTIST CHURCH

IF YOU KNOW THE AUTHOR, YOU WILL LOVE HIS BOOK

THE REAL VICTORY OF FAITH IS TO TRUST GOD IN THE DARK

THE
GREATER ANTIOCH
MISSIONARY BAPTIST
CHURCH

A SMALL GOOD DEED
IS BETTER THAN A
LARGE GOOD
INTENTION

CALVARY
BAPTIST

A GOOD ATTITUDE
TOWARD LIFE
BEGINS WITH GRATTITUDE
TOWARD GOD

PRAY FOR A GOOD
HARVEST BUT
CONTINUE TO HOE.

Celeste Road
Church of God
PASTOR: MUSIC:

WE SERVE A GOD
WHO DOES THE
IMPOSSIBLE

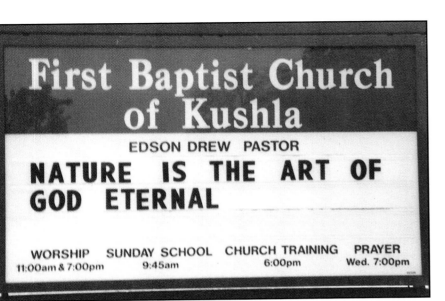

First Baptist Church of Kushla

EDSON DREW PASTOR

NATURE IS THE ART OF GOD ETERNAL

| WORSHIP | SUNDAY SCHOOL | CHURCH TRAINING | PRAYER |
| 11:00am & 7:00pm | 9:45am | 6:00pm | Wed. 7:00pm |

CHURCH OF CHRIST

SPANISH FORT, ALABAMA

SUNDAY:
BIBLE STUDY 9:00 AM
MORNING WORSHIP 10:00 AM
EVENING WORSHIP 6:00 PM

WEDNESDAY:
BIBLE STUDY 7:00 PM
MINISTER:
MAX McCLENDON

MEEKNESS IS NOT WEAKNESS

First Church of the Nazarene

THE BEST ANGLE FROM WHICH TO APPROACH ANY PROBLEM IS THE TRY-ANGLE

A LITTLE LIGHT IN A DARK PLACE SERVES A GREAT PURPOSE

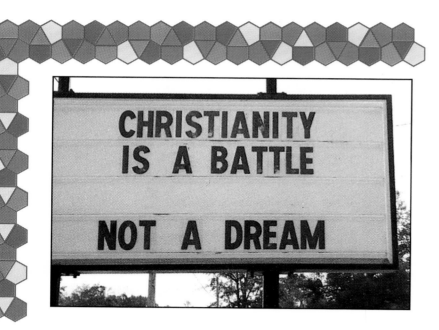

CHRISTIANITY
IS A BATTLE

NOT A DREAM

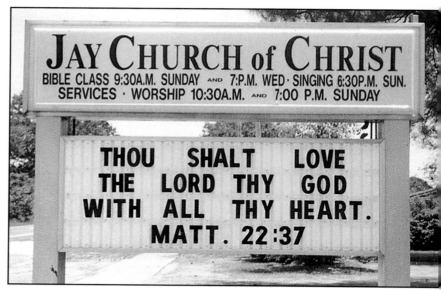

JAY CHURCH of CHRIST
BIBLE CLASS 9:30A.M. SUNDAY AND 7:P.M. WED · SINGING 6:30P.M. SUN.
SERVICES · WORSHIP 10:30A.M. AND 7:00 P.M. SUNDAY

THOU SHALT LOVE
THE LORD THY GOD
WITH ALL THY HEART.
MATT. 22:37

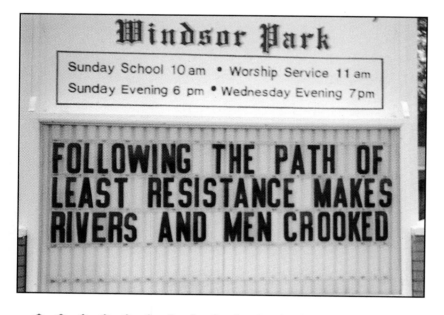

Windsor Park
Sunday School 10 am · Worship Service 11 am
Sunday Evening 6 pm · Wednesday Evening 7pm

FOLLOWING THE PATH OF
LEAST RESISTANCE MAKES
RIVERS AND MEN CROOKED

GOD IS MORE INTERESTED
IN YOUR AVAILABILITY
THAN IN YOUR ABILITY
WELCOME

FIRST ASSEMBLY OF GOD

NO GOD - NO PEACE
KNOW GOD - KNOW PEACE!

SUNDAY SCHOOL 9:45AM   WORSHIP 11:00 AM 6:00PM   WED EVE 7:00 PM

IS YOUR HOME ON THE ROCK OR ROCKS

HELP NEEDED

WESTERN HILLS Church of Christ

A DEAD CHRISTIAN
HAS MORE LIFE
IN DEATH THAN
HE HAD IN LIFE

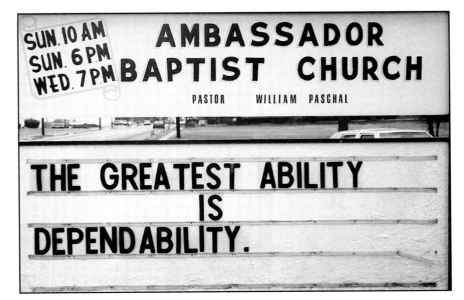

SUN. 10 AM
SUN. 6 PM
WED. 7 PM

AMBASSADOR BAPTIST CHURCH

PASTOR   WILLIAM PASCHAL

THE GREATEST ABILITY
IS
DEPENDABILITY.

First Baptist Church

PEACE IS NOT MADE IN DOCUMENTS, BUT IN THE HEARTS OF PEOPLE

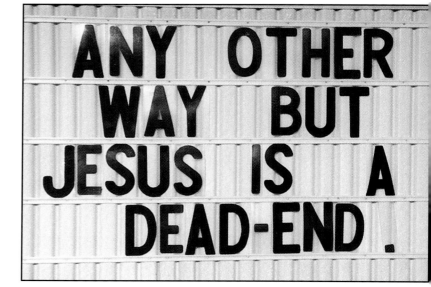

ANY OTHER WAY BUT JESUS IS A DEAD-END.

A WELL-READ BIBLE IS THE SIGN OF A WELL-FED SOUL.

FIRST ASSEMBLY of GOD

FAULTS ARE THICK WHEN

LOVE IS THIN

Moffat Road
Assembly of God

THERE IS A WAY TO
STAY OUT OF HELL,
BUT NO WAY TO GET
OUT OF HELL.

Assembly of God
TABERNACLE

SUNDAY SCHOOL   WORSHIP   WED.
9:45AM   10:30AM & 6:00PM   7:00PM

THE FAMILY ALTAR
WOULD ALTER
MANY   A   FAMILY !
PASTOR RANDY COMER

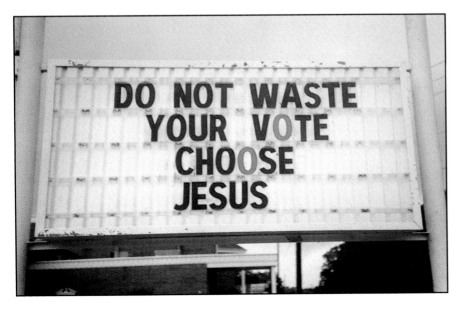

DO NOT WASTE
YOUR VOTE
CHOOSE
JESUS

FIRST BAPTIST CHURCH
— STATE LINE, MS. —

IF YOU WANT TO WALK
WITH GOD YOU MUST
GO GOD'S WAY
S.S. 10-00 AM   D.T. 6-00 PM

LIFE IS SHORT
DEATH IS SURE
SIN THE CAUSE
CHRIST THE CURE

EVANGEL TEMPLE
ASSEMBLY
OF GOD
FREDDY CARTER
A GOOD LAUGH IS
SUNSHINE IN A HOME

First
Baptist Church
OF HOLT, FLORIDA
A SOUTHERN BAPTIST CHURCH   TERRY FLOYD PASTOR
LOVE NOT ONLY
GIVES, IT
ALSO FORGIVES
COLOSSIANS 3.13

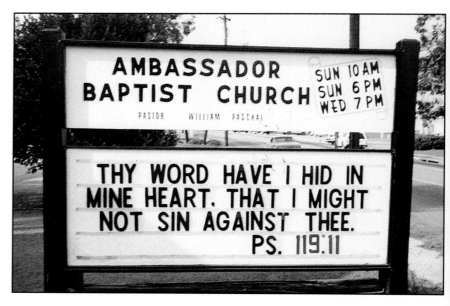

AMBASSADOR   SUN 10AM
BAPTIST CHURCH   SUN 6PM
PASTOR   WILLIAM PASCHAL   WED 7PM
THY WORD HAVE I HID IN
MINE HEART. THAT I MIGHT
NOT SIN AGAINST THEE.
PS. 119:11

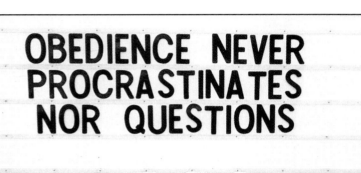

OBEDIENCE NEVER PROCRASTINATES NOR QUESTIONS

THE KEY TO SPIRITUAL FITNESS IS FORGIVENESS

CALVARY BAPTIST

GOD DOESN'T USE AN ANSWERING MACHINE HE TAKES EACH CALL PERSONALLY

CHRISTLIKENESS IS NEVER OUT OF STYLE.

THE SALVATION ARMY
COMMUNITY WORSHIP CENTER

*A PSALM A DAY
KEEPS THE DEVIL AWAY*

GOD HAS TWO HOMES
ONE IS HEAVEN
ONE THE THANKFUL HEART

Celeste Road
Church of God

PASTOR: MUSIC:

HEAVEN IS A PREPARED
PLACE
FOR PREPARED PEOPLE

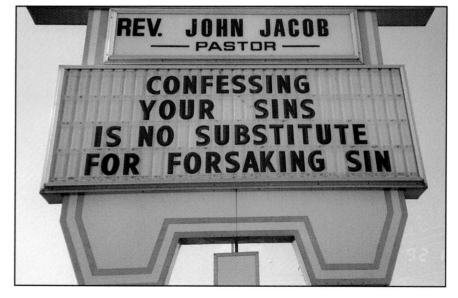

REV. JOHN JACOB
—— PASTOR ——

CONFESSING
YOUR SINS
IS NO SUBSTITUTE
FOR FORSAKING SIN

ZION BAPTIST CHURCH

GOD DOES NOT
MAKE SINNERS
HE FORGIVES THEM

REV. KENNETH FARLEY

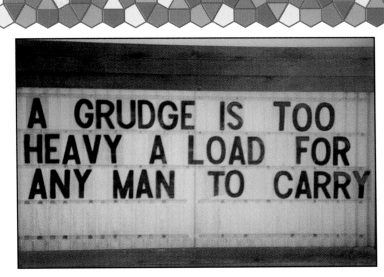

A GRUDGE IS TOO
HEAVY A LOAD FOR
ANY MAN TO CARRY

Bible Missionary Church

HOWEVER DEATH FINDS
YOU ETERNITY WILL
KEEP YOU

MOVELLA
ASSEMBLY OF GOD

SINCERITY IS AN
OPENNESS OF HEART

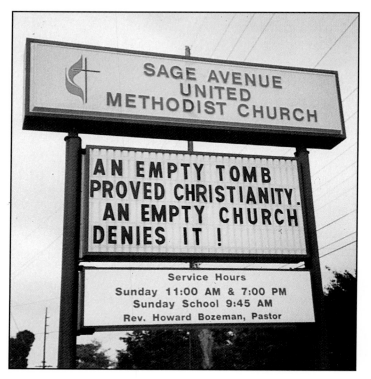

SAGE AVENUE
UNITED
METHODIST CHURCH

AN EMPTY TOMB
PROVED CHRISTIANITY.
AN EMPTY CHURCH
DENIES IT !

Service Hours
Sunday 11:00 AM & 7:00 PM
Sunday School 9:45 AM
Rev. Howard Bozeman, Pastor

ORCHARD BAPTIST CHURCH

THE TEN COMMANDMENTS
ARE NOT
MULTIPLE CHOICE

WHEN YOUR
KNEES KNOCK,
TRY KNEELING
ON THEM.

YOU'RE NEVER A
LOSER UNTIL
YOU QUIT TRYING

GLENCOE CUMBERLAND PRESBYTERIAN

WORK IS LOVE MADE VISIBLE

WESTERN HILLS Church of Christ

SELF SURRENDER IS THE KEY OF LIFE

CALVARY BAPTIST

NOTHING CAN HAPPEN TO YOU TODAY THAT YOU & GOD CAN'T HANDLE

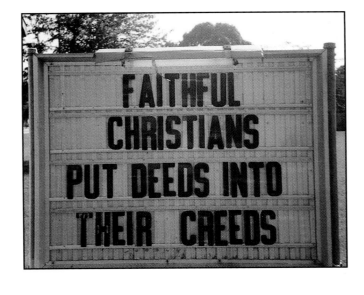

FAITHFUL CHRISTIANS PUT DEEDS INTO THEIR CREEDS

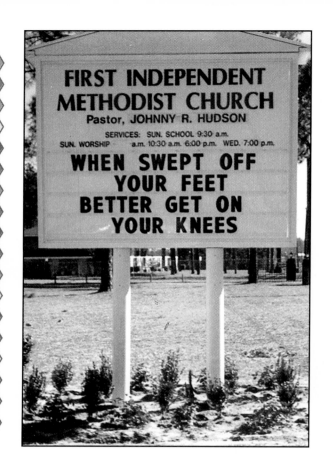

FIRST INDEPENDENT
METHODIST CHURCH
Pastor, JOHNNY R. HUDSON

SERVICES: SUN. SCHOOL 9:30 a.m.
SUN. WORSHIP   a.m. 10:30 a.m. 6:00 p.m. WED. 7:00 p.m.

WHEN SWEPT OFF
YOUR FEET
BETTER GET ON
YOUR KNEES

THOSE WHO WOULD
RULE MEN MUST
BE RULED BY
GOD

WHEN IT SEEMS
THERE IS
NO WAY OUT
LET
CHRIST IN

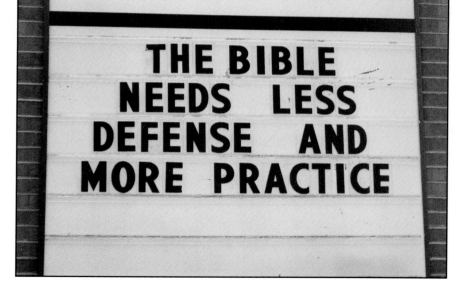

THE BIBLE
NEEDS LESS
DEFENSE AND
MORE PRACTICE

Straight Way CHURCH Of The Lord Jesus Christ

LIFE IS FRAGILE HANDLE WITH PRAYER

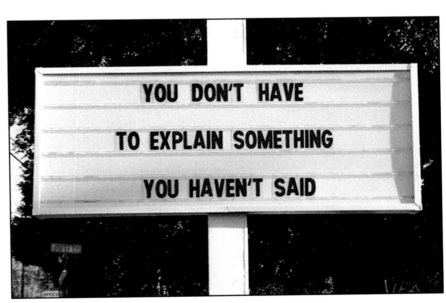

YOU DON'T HAVE

TO EXPLAIN SOMETHING

YOU HAVEN'T SAID

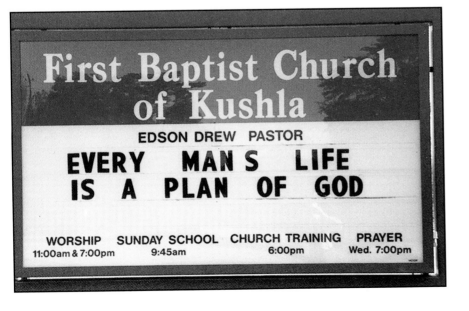

First Baptist Church of Kushla

EDSON DREW PASTOR

EVERY MANS LIFE IS A PLAN OF GOD

WORSHIP 11:00am & 7:00pm SUNDAY SCHOOL 9:45am CHURCH TRAINING 6:00pm PRAYER Wed. 7:00pm

Bible Missionary Church

WHEN CHRIST RULES THE HEART PEACE RULES THE DAY

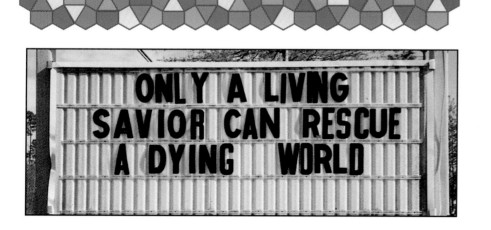

ONLY A LIVING SAVIOR CAN RESCUE A DYING WORLD

ZION BAPTIST CHURCH

GOD FORGIVES SINNERS BUT DOES NOT MAKE THEM

REV. KENNETH FARLEY

FIRST BAPTIST CHURCH

THE LORD MAY CALM YOUR STORM BUT MORE OFTEN HE'LL CALM YOU

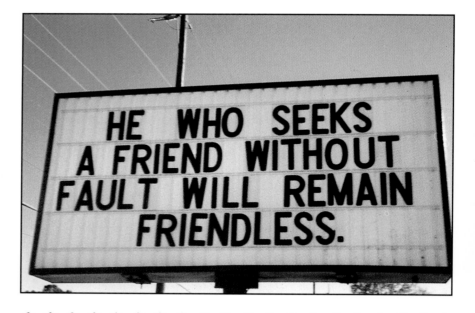

HE WHO SEEKS A FRIEND WITHOUT FAULT WILL REMAIN FRIENDLESS.

First Church of the Nazarene

LITTLE IS MUCH

WHEN GOD IS IN IT

NO PERSON CAN
CHOOSE NOT TO BE
THE OBJECT
OF GOD'S LOVE.

MEMORIAL
METHODIST
HAPPINESS IS LIKE JAM
IF YOU SPREAD IT.
IT WILL GET ON YOU

Celeste Road
Church of God
PASTOR: MUSIC:

SWALLOWING
PRIDE IS
NONFATTING

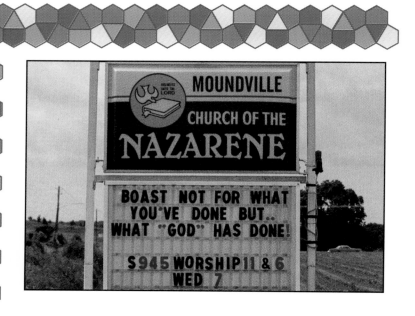

MOUNDVILLE
CHURCH OF THE
NAZARENE

BOAST NOT FOR WHAT
YOU'VE DONE BUT..
WHAT "GOD" HAS DONE!

S 945 WORSHIP 11 & 6
WED 7

NEVER LET
YESTERDAY
USE UP
TODAY.

IF GOD SENDS US,
HE ALSO GOES
WITH US.

WALTER HILL
FIRST BAPTIST CHURCH
TRESPASSERS
WILL BE FORGIVEN
ON SITE!

CALVARY BAPTIST

WHEN IN DOUBT OF GOD'S LOVE FOR YOU - READ JOHN 3:16

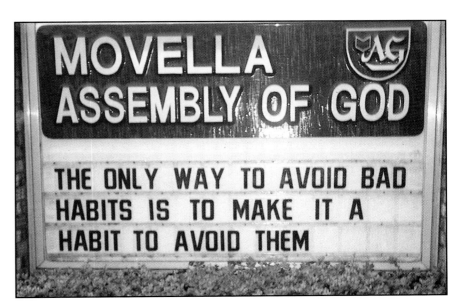

MOVELLA ASSEMBLY OF GOD

THE ONLY WAY TO AVOID BAD HABITS IS TO MAKE IT A HABIT TO AVOID THEM

Old Spanish Fort BAPTIST CHURCH
← NEXT LEFT

UNLESS YOU'RE A RABBIT DON'T PUT MUCH FAITH IN A RABBITS FOOT
WORSHIP 830 1100 630

7100

Moffat Road Assembly of God

WHEN YOUR BACK'S AGAINST THE WALL, REMEMBER HIS WAS AGAINST THE CROSS

TO HEAR
THE CALL OF GOD
ONE MUST BE IN
HEARING DISTANCE

A WARM SMILE
THAWS
AN ICY STARE

IT IS NEVER
WRONG TO GET
EVEN WITH
SOMEONE WHO
HAS HELPED YOU

FRIENDSHIP
BAPTIST CHURCH

SUNDAY SCHOOL
10:00AM

WORSHIP
11:00AM & 7:00PM

KEITH D. SWARTZ
Pastor

WE'RE A CHURCH
OWNED & OPERATED
BY JESUS CHRIST!

THE GREATER ANTIOCH MISSIONARY BAPTIST CHURCH
DR. JOHN W. DAVIS, SR — PASTOR

DON'T BREAK THE BRIDGE YOU MUST CROSS BY FAILING TO FORGIVE

First Church of the Nazarene

HAPPINESS

IS AN INSIDE JOB

GOD JUDGES MAN
AFTER HE DIES
MEN START
MUCH EARLIER

SUN. 10 AM
SUN. 6 PM
WED. 7 PM

AMBASSADOR BAPTIST CHURCH

PASTOR   WILLIAM PASCHAL

O GOD, THOU ART MY GOD;
EARLY WILL I SEEK THEE...
PS. 63:1

Moffat Road Assembly of God

GOD'S WAYS ARE BEHIND THE SCENES, BUT HE MOVES ALL THE SCENES HE IS BEHIND

WRONG IS WRONG REGARDLESS OF WHO ELSE IS DOING IT

FORESTHILL CHURCH OF GOD

OVERLOOK THE FAULTS OF OTHERS BUT LOOK OVER YOUR OWN CAREFULLY

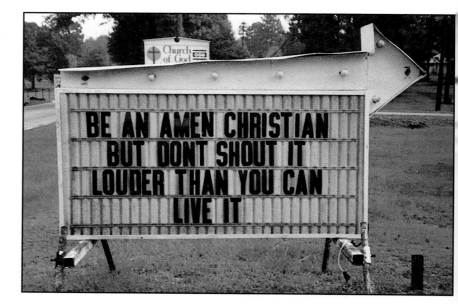

BE AN AMEN CHRISTIAN BUT DONT SHOUT IT LOUDER THAN YOU CAN LIVE IT

GOD CAN USE
REVERSES TO MOVE
US FORWARD

SIN IS NEVER
WORTH
THE TROUBLE
PSALM 62.10

FIRST
ASSEMBLY of GOD

THERE IS NO PILLOW
SO SOFT AS A
CLEAR CONSCIENCE

WELCOME
First Assembly of God

DARKER THE
NIGHT
THE BRIGHTER
THE LIGHT SHINES

SUN. SCHOOL 9:45 A.M.
WORSHIP 10:45 A.M.
SUN. EVE. 6:00 P.M.
WED. 7:00 P.M.

REV. KENNETH MORRIS: PASTOR

SOME MINDS ARE LIKE CONCRETE... THOROUGHLY MIXED & PERMANENTLY SET.

First Baptist Church
Rev. J.H. WILLIAMS
PASTOR

STRENGTH IN PRAYER IS BETTER THAN LENGTH IN PRAYER

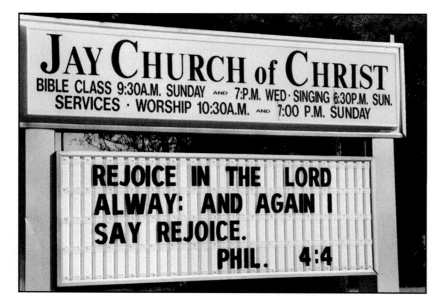

JAY CHURCH of CHRIST
BIBLE CLASS 9:30A.M. SUNDAY AND 7:P.M. WED· SINGING 6:30P.M. SUN. SERVICES · WORSHIP 10:30A.M. AND 7:00 P.M. SUNDAY

REJOICE IN THE LORD ALWAY: AND AGAIN I SAY REJOICE.
PHIL. 4:4

SO, YOU BELIEVE IN GOD, FUNNY SO DOES THE DEVIL!

TO ERR
MEANS
YOU'RE
TRYING.

BELLVIEW
ASSEMBLY
OF GOD

SALVATION
IS FOR TIME
AND ETERNITY

D.B. GREEN, PASTOR

Wesley Memorial
United Methodist Church

FORBIDDEN FRUIT
MAKES
FOR A
BAD JAM

First Baptist Church of Kushla

EDSON DREW PASTOR

A MAN OF COURAGE IS
ALSO FULL OF FAITH

WORSHIP	SUNDAY SCHOOL	CHURCH TRAINING	PRAYER
11:00am & 7:00pm	9:45am	6:00pm	Wed. 7:00pm

FELLOWSHIP
BAPTIST CHURCH

THE SINS OF OTHERS
ALWAYS SEEMS
GREATER THAN
OUR OWN

WAYNE COUNTY
BAPTIST
ASSOCIATION

A HAPPY MARRIAGE
IS THE UNION OF
TWO FORGIVERS

FIRST BAPTIST CHURCH

OUR CHILDREN ARE
LIKE MIRRORS
THEY REFLECT OUR
ATTIUDES IN LIFE

DR. DAVID K. HINSON, PASTOR
SUNDAY SERVICES
MORNING WORSHIP 9:00am & 11:00am • BIBLE STUDY 9:45am • EVENING WORSHIP 6:00pm

SAGE AVENUE
UNITED
METHODIST CHURCH

GOD'S
RETIREMENT PLAN
IS OUT OF
THIS WORLD

Service Hours
Sunday 11:00 AM & 6:00 PM
Sunday School 9:45 AM
Rev. Howard Bozeman, Pastor

BEATLINE BAPTIST CHURCH

TO BELITTLE
IS TO
BE LITTLE

ELBA UNITED METHODIST CHURCH

ELBA HAS SO
MUCH TO BE
THANKFUL
FOR !

REV. WINSTON JAY
10:50 A.M 6:00 P.M.

PASTOR
JAMES PREUETT

Gulfcrest Baptist Church

KIND ACTIONS BEGIN
WITH KIND THOUGHTS

IF YOU'VE BEGUN THE
DANCE WITH THE
LORD DON'T EVER
CHANGE PARTNERS!

The CHRISTIAN LIGHTHOUSE
• PASTOR TERRY HOSMER •
Sunday School 10ᵃᵐ | Sunday Evening 6ᵖᵐ
Sunday Worship 11ᵃᵐ | Wednesday Evening 7ᵖᵐ

SEASON
EVERYTHING
WITH
LOVE

MOVELLA
ASSEMBLY OF GOD

ONE CAN CONQUER A BAD
HABIT EASIER TODAY THAN
TOMORROW

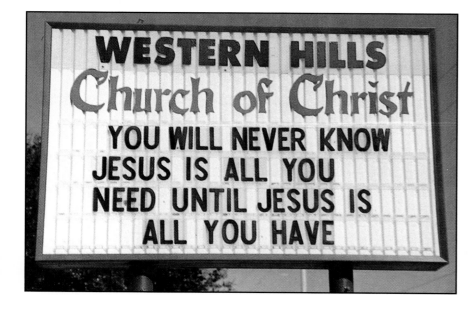

WESTERN HILLS
Church of Christ
YOU WILL NEVER KNOW
JESUS IS ALL YOU
NEED UNTIL JESUS IS
ALL YOU HAVE

TOMORROW'S EVENTS
MAY RESULT FROM
TODAY'S PRAYERS.

LOVE IS A HAMMER
THAT WILL BREAK
THE HARDEST HEART

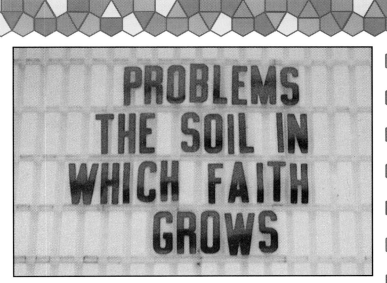

PROBLEMS
THE SOIL IN
WHICH FAITH
GROWS

LIBERTY
Assembly of God

" TRUE LOVE"
CAN BE FOUND IN
JESUS CHRIST

AMBASSADOR
BAPTIST CHURCH
PASTOR WILLIAM PASCHAL

SUN. 10 AM
SUN. 6 PM
WED. 7 PM

BECAUSE OF GOD'S GRACE
FAILURE IS NEVER
FINAL

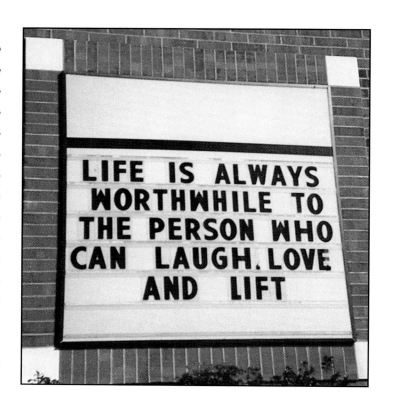

LIFE IS ALWAYS
WORTHWHILE TO
THE PERSON WHO
CAN LAUGH. LOVE
AND LIFT

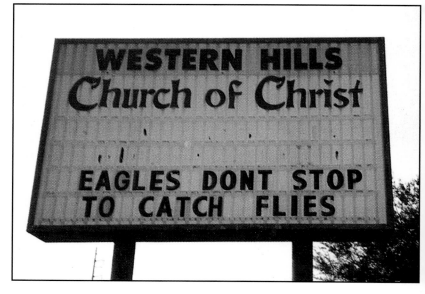

WESTERN HILLS
Church of Christ

EAGLES DONT STOP
TO CATCH FLIES

MOVELLA
ASSEMBLY OF GOD

A SOFT ANSWER HAS OFTEN
BEEN THE MEANS OF
BREAKING A HARD HEART

CENTRAL
CHURCH OF CHRIST

IF GOD IS
YOUR CO-PILOT
YOU
NEED TO CHANGE
SEATS

KELLY WHEELER - MINISTER

ZION BAPTIST CHURCH

EXPERIENCE:
COMPLUSORY EDUCATION

REV. KENNETH FARLEY

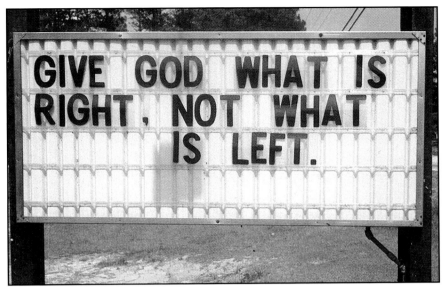

GIVE GOD WHAT IS
RIGHT, NOT WHAT
IS LEFT.

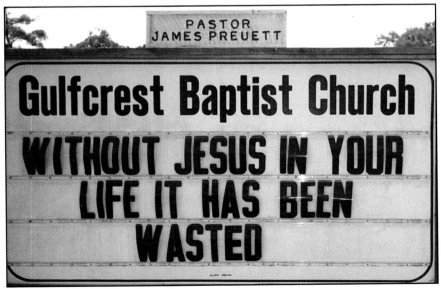

PASTOR
JAMES PREUETT

Gulfcrest Baptist Church

WITHOUT JESUS IN YOUR
LIFE IT HAS BEEN
WASTED

Moffat Road
Assembly of God

"LOVE FOR GOD"

NOT JUST A FEELING
IT'S A COMMITMENT

THE THINGS YOU FEAR
THE MOST IN YOUR LIFE.
FEARS GOD

WAYNE COUNTY
BAPTIST
ASSOCIATION

HOT HEADS AND
COLD HEARTS
NEVER SOLVE
ANYTHING

Fellowship
Church

GOD'S METHODS MAY
CHANGE BUT HE
DOES NOT

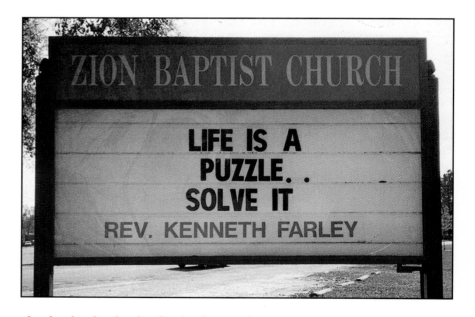

ZION BAPTIST CHURCH

LIFE IS A
PUZZLE. .
SOLVE IT
REV. KENNETH FARLEY

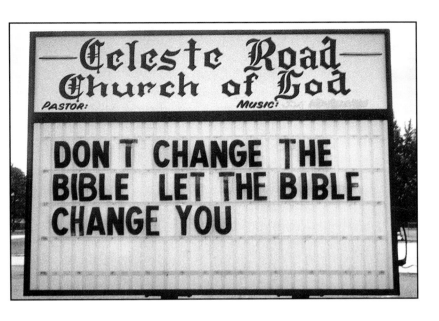

Celeste Road
Church of God

PASTOR: MUSIC:

DON'T CHANGE THE
BIBLE LET THE BIBLE
CHANGE YOU

FIRST
BAPTIST CHURCH

FEAR KNOCKED AT THE
DOOR FAITH ANSWERED
NO ONE WAS THERE

WELCOME
SOUTHERN ✝ BAPTIST

FIRST BAPTIST
CHURCH

SUNDAY   SUNDAY 8:30&11:00 A.M.   CHURCH 5:45   WEDNESDAY
SCHOOL   WORSHIP   7:00 P.M.   TRAINING P.M. PRAYER MEETING

COMPASSION
IS
LOVE IN ACTION

JESUS CHRIST IS LORD
OVER COVINGTON COUNTY &
ALABAMA

SOUTH SIDE
CHURCH OF CHRIST

APPLY BIBLE TEACHING
TO
YOUR LIFE EVERY DAY!

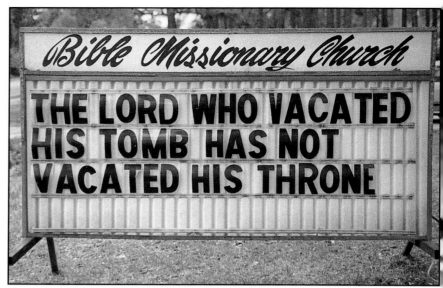

Bible Missionary Church

THE LORD WHO VACATED
HIS TOMB HAS NOT
VACATED HIS THRONE

MOVELLA
ASSEMBLY OF GOD

THE ROAD TO SUCCESS
IS ALWAYS
UNDER CONSTRUCTION

FIRST BAPTIST
CHURCH
OF THEODORE

THINK
SELDOM OF ENEMIES
OFTEN OF FRIENDS
ALWAYS OF CHRIST

SUNDAY   WEDNESDAY
SUNDAY SCHOOL 9:30AM   DISCIPLESHIP TRAINING 6:00PM   PRAYER SERVICE 7:00PM
MORNING WORSHIP 10:50AM   EVENING WORSHIP 7:00PM

PASTOR
LONNIE B. BYRD

ORCHARD BAPTIST CHURCH

MONEY TALKS
BUT
NOT IN ETERINTY.

SOLID ROCK
BAPTIST
CHURCH

PASTOR JERRY WAYNE GOSS

HELP
IF YOU REALLY WANT HELP
CALL 1-800-JESUS!

Old Spanish Fort
BAPTIST CHURCH
NEXT RIGHT →

A FRIEND
IS ONE WHO KNOWS YOU
AND
STILL LIKES YOU

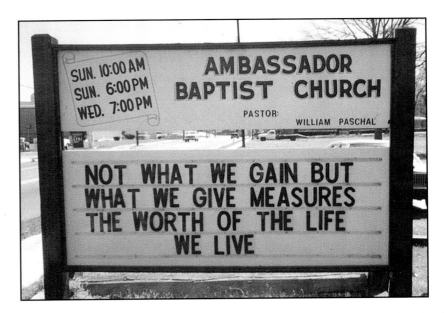

SUN. 10:00 AM
SUN. 6:00 PM
WED. 7:00 PM

AMBASSADOR
BAPTIST CHURCH
PASTOR:
WILLIAM PASCHAL

NOT WHAT WE GAIN BUT
WHAT WE GIVE MEASURES
THE WORTH OF THE LIFE
WE LIVE

LIVING FAITH BAPTIST CHURCH

WHATEVER YOUR PAST
HAS BEEN
YOU HAVE A
SPOTLESS FUTURE

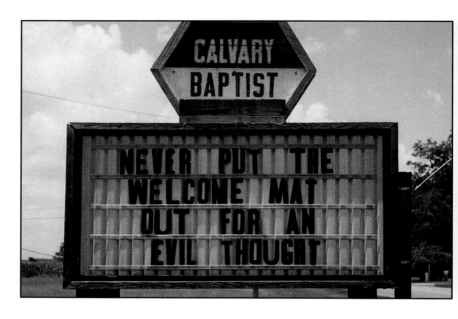

CALVARY BAPTIST

NEVER PUT THE
WELCOME MAT
OUT FOR AN
EVIL THOUGHT

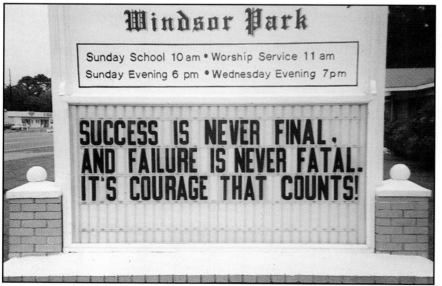

Windsor Park

Sunday School 10 am • Worship Service 11 am
Sunday Evening 6 pm • Wednesday Evening 7pm

SUCCESS IS NEVER FINAL,
AND FAILURE IS NEVER FATAL.
IT'S COURAGE THAT COUNTS!

AMBASSADOR BAPTIST CHURCH

SUN. 10 AM
SUN. 6 PM
WED. 7 PM

PASTOR   WILLIAM   PASCHAL

FAITHFULNESS IS NOT
A REQUEST BUT GOD'S
COMMAND.

Celeste Road
Church of God
PASTOR: Music:

DID YOU KNOW
THAT HEB. 9:27
MEANS YOU?

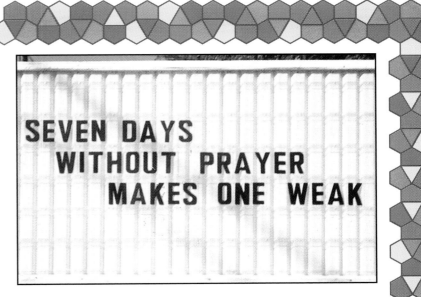

SEVEN DAYS
WITHOUT PRAYER
MAKES ONE WEAK

Abundant Life
ASSEMBLY OF GOD

THE MOST DIFFICULT THING
TO GIVE AWAY IS KINDNESS -
IT'S USUALLY RETURNED.

WESTERN HILLS
Church of Christ

WHERE THERES A WILL
THERES A WONT

TEMPLE BAPTIST CHURCH

DONT POINT A FINGER
LEND A HAND
SUNDAY SCHOOL 10:00AM
WORSHIP 11:00AM-6:00PM
WEDNESDAY 7:00PM
BILL ADAMS, PASTOR

FIRST BAPTIST CHURCH OF THEODORE

THE WISDOM OF THE AGES
THE HOLY BIBLE

SUNDAY
SUNDAY SCHOOL 9:30AM   DISCIPLESHIP TRAINING 6:00PM
MORNING WORSHIP 10:50AM   EVENING WORSHIP 7:00PM

WEDNESDAY
PRAYER SERVICE 7:00PM

PASTOR
LONNIE R BYRD

SAGE AVENUE UNITED METHODIST CHURCH

CHRIST WANTS YOU TO MEET HIM AT A CHURCH OF YOUR CHOICE!

BIBLE BAPTIST CHURCH

CHRISTIANS WHO ARE WORTH THEIR SALT WILL MAKE OTHERS THIRSTY

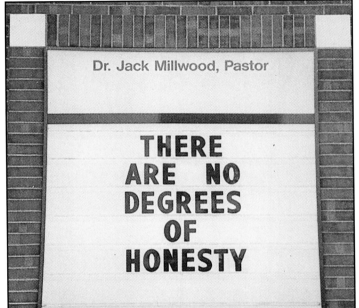

Dr. Jack Millwood, Pastor

THERE
ARE NO
DEGREES
OF
HONESTY

CHURCH OF GOD

HURTS ARE HEALED
AT GOD'S ALTAR

WELCOME

GOOD
SHEPHERD
LUTHERAN
CHURCH

WORSHIP   8:00 AM
EDUCATION   10:45 AM
HOUR   9:30 AM

SEEK FIRST
THE KINGDOM
OF GOD

TURN YOUR
TROUBLES OVER
TO GOD HE IS MORE
TRUST WORTHY
PSALMS 7

Bible Missionary Church

THERE IS BUT A STEP BETWEEN ME AND DEATH

FORESTHILL CHURCH OF GOD

DEAD NOSES
SMELL NO ROSES
GIVE THEM NOW!

Ernest L. Quinley - Pastor

AMBASSADOR BAPTIST CHURCH

SUN. 10 AM
SUN. 6 PM
WED. 7 PM

PASTOR WILLIAM PASCHAL

CHRIST WAS DELIVERED FOR OUR SINS THAT WE MIGHT BE DELIVERED FROM OUR SINS

MOVELLA ASSEMBLY OF GOD

LYING IS A HANDLE THAT FITS ALL THE DEVIL'S TOOLS

WESTERN HILLS
Church of Christ

WE TAKE TIME FOR
ANYTHING WE REALLY
CARE ABOUT

GULF COAST
BAPTIST TEMPLE

JESUS IS THE LIGHT
OF THE WORLD AND HE
NEVER GOES OUT

SAGE AVENUE
UNITED
METHODIST CHURCH

DEEP INSIDE YOUR
SOUL GOD IS
QUIETLY
WAITING !

Service Hours
Sunday 11:00 AM & 6:00 PM
Sunday School 9:45 AM
Rev. Howard Bozeman, Pastor

TO GET BACK
ON YOUR FEET:
START DOWN
ON YOUR KNEES!

AMBASSADOR BAPTIST CHURCH

SUN 10 AM
SUN 6 PM
WED 7 PM

IT IS FAR BETTER TO STAND FOR SOMETHING THAN TO FALL FOR ANYTHING!

WALTER HILL FIRST BAPTIST CHURCH

GOD GAVE MOSES 10 COMMANDMENTS NOT 10 SUGGESTIONS !

WORK WITHOUT WORSHIP MEANS WORRY

GOD'S HELP IS ONLY A PRAYER AWAY

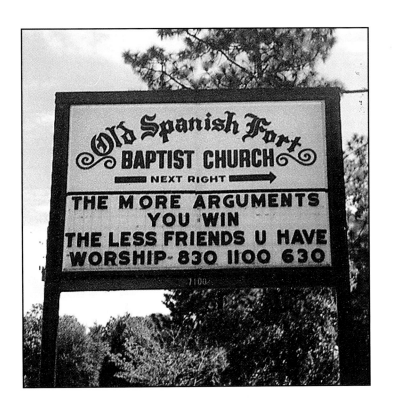

Old Spanish Fort
BAPTIST CHURCH
→ NEXT RIGHT →

THE MORE ARGUMENTS
YOU WIN
THE LESS FRIENDS U HAVE
WORSHIP- 830 1100 630

Celeste Road
Church of God
PASTOR: MUSIC:

IF YOU ARE SEATED IN
HEAVENLY PLACES,
SIT STILL

✝ PLAINWAY
BAPTIST
CHURCH

NO   PROBLEM
IS   TOO BIG
FOR   GOD

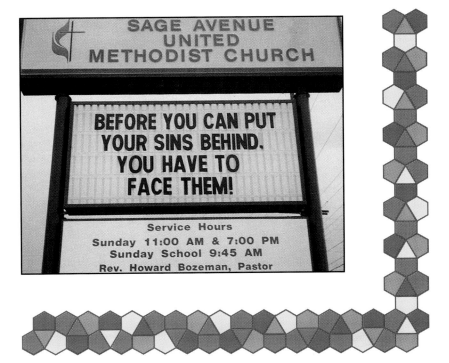

SAGE AVENUE
UNITED
METHODIST CHURCH

BEFORE YOU CAN PUT
YOUR SINS BEHIND,
YOU HAVE TO
FACE THEM!

Service Hours
Sunday 11:00 AM & 7:00 PM
Sunday School 9:45 AM
Rev. Howard Bozeman, Pastor

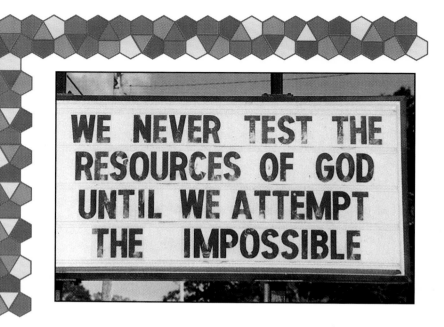

WE NEVER TEST THE
RESOURCES OF GOD
UNTIL WE ATTEMPT
THE IMPOSSIBLE

LOVE IS A
LITTLE WORD-PEOPLE
MAKE IT BIG.

Celeste Road
Church of God

PASTOR: MUSIC:

THE FUTURE DESTINY
OF THE CHILD IS ALWAYS
THE WORK OF THE
MOTHER

A FRIEND
LISTENS
WITH THE
HEART.

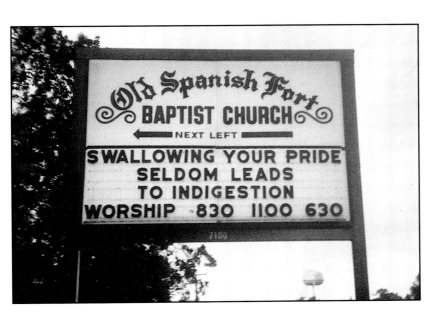

Old Spanish Fort
BAPTIST CHURCH
◄══ NEXT LEFT ══►
SWALLOWING YOUR PRIDE
SELDOM LEADS
TO INDIGESTION
WORSHIP 830 1100 630

First Baptist
Church
Rev. J.H. WILLIAMS
PASTOR

NEVER BE AFRAID TO
TRUST AN UNKOWN
FUTURE TO A
KNOWN GOD

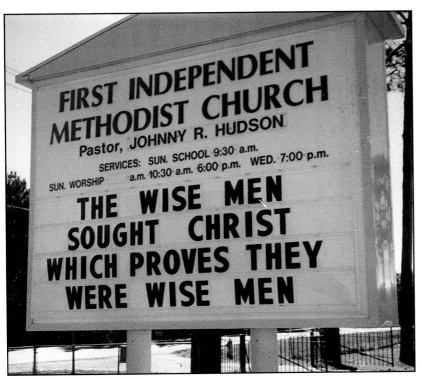

FIRST INDEPENDENT
METHODIST CHURCH
Pastor, JOHNNY R. HUDSON
SERVICES: SUN. SCHOOL 9:30 a.m.
SUN. WORSHIP   a.m. 10:30 a.m. 6:00 p.m.   WED. 7:00 p.m.

THE WISE MEN
SOUGHT CHRIST
WHICH PROVES THEY
WERE WISE MEN

Gulfcrest Baptist Church
BURDENS SHOULD NEVER
GET US DOWN EXCEPT
ON OUR KNEES TO PRAY

SUNDAY CLEARS AWAY THE RUST OF THE WEEK.

First Baptist Church of Kushla

EDSON DREW PASTOR

GOD SOMETIMES PUTS US ON OUR BACKS SO THAT WE MAY LOOK UPWARD

WORSHIP	SUNDAY SCHOOL	CHURCH TRAINING	PRAYER
11:00am & 7:00pm	9:45am	6:00pm	Wed. 7:00pm

HERITAGE BAPTIST CHURCH
OF PENSACOLA

SUNDAY SCHOOL	WORSHIP	WED.	JERALD L. MANLEY
9:30AM	10:00AM & 6:00PM	7:00PM	Pastor

NO ONE IS RICH ENOUGH TO BUY BACK THE PAST

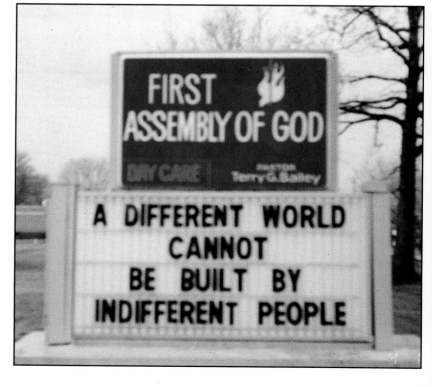

FIRST ASSEMBLY OF GOD

DAY CARE
Terry G. Bailey

A DIFFERENT WORLD CANNOT BE BUILT BY INDIFFERENT PEOPLE

UNITED PENTECOSTAL CHURCH

C.E. CALK
PASTOR

WELCOME !

RESURRECTION - A
GLORIOUS NEW BIRTH
& WONDERFUL NEW LIFE

SOUTH SIDE
CHURCH OF CHRIST

WE MUST BELIEVE IN GOD

TO BELIEVE HIS WORD

IT IS GOOD TO
SING PRAISES
UNTO OUR GOD

NEVER TAKE ON MORE
RESPONSIBILITIES
THAN YOU HAVE TIME
TO PRAY ABOUT

"MOTHER"
ANOTHER NAME FOR
LOVE!

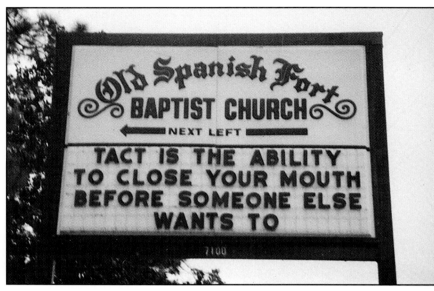

Old Spanish Fort
BAPTIST CHURCH
← NEXT LEFT →
TACT IS THE ABILITY
TO CLOSE YOUR MOUTH
BEFORE SOMEONE ELSE
WANTS TO

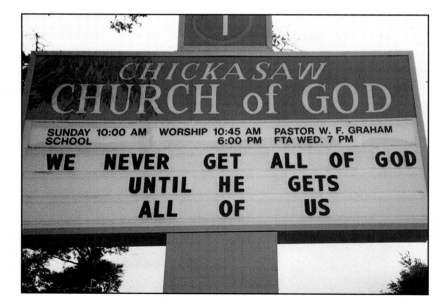

CHICKASAW
CHURCH of GOD
SUNDAY SCHOOL 10:00 AM   WORSHIP 10:45 AM 6:00 PM   PASTOR W. F. GRAHAM FTA WED. 7 PM
WE   NEVER   GET   ALL   OF   GOD
UNTIL   HE   GETS
ALL   OF   US

WATCH YOUR
THOUGHTS THEY MAY
BECOME WORDS
ANY MINUTE

CHURCH OF GOD

YOU NEVER GET A SECOND CHANCE TO MAKE A GOOD FIRST IMPRESSION

WESTERN HILLS Church of Christ
THE GOOD MAN YOU CAN'T KEEP DOWN IS PROBABLY ON THE UP AND UP

FIND OUT WHERE GOD IS WORKING AND JOIN HIM

SUNDAY
SUNDAY SCHOOL 9:30AM   DISCIPLESHIP TRAINING 6:00PM
MORNING WORSHIP 10:50AM   EVENING WORSHIP 7:00PM

WEDNESDAY
PRAYER SERVICE 7:00PM

FIRST ASSEMBLY of GOD
THE WORST PRISON IS
A CLOSED HEART

CALVARY DELIVERANCE TEMPLE

THE YOKE OF THE LORD WILL NOT FIT A STIFF NECK

Celeste Road Church of God

PASTOR: MUSIC:

IT WASN'T RAINING WHEN NOAH BUILT THE ARK... ARE YOU READY?

FRIENDSHIP BAPTIST CHURCH

SUNDAY SCHOOL 10:00AM   WORSHIP 11:00AM & 7:00PM   KEITH D. SWARTZ Pastor

GOD IS LOVE THE DEVIL HATE: WHO DO YOU SERVE?

THE GREATER ANTIOCH MISSIONARY BAPTIST CHURCH
DR. JOHN W. BLANDIN, PASTOR

GOD'S WRATH COMES BY MEASURE HIS GRACE WITHOUT MEASURE

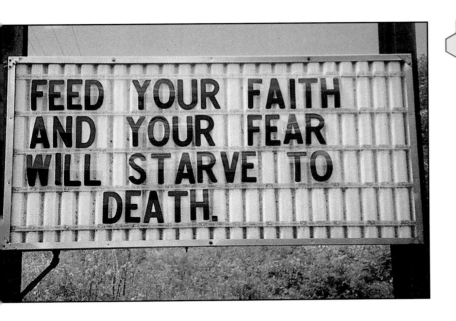

FEED YOUR FAITH AND YOUR FEAR WILL STARVE TO DEATH.

LOVE DOES NOT DOMINATE IT CULTIVATES

PLEASANT VALLEY CHURCH OF CHRIST

MANY BELIEVE IN GOD

BUT NOT MANY BELIEVE GOD

GARY C. HAMPTON, MINISTER

MILES H. MAYO ASSOC. MINISTER

Munford BAPTIST CHURCH

THE BIBLE PROMISES NO LOAVES TO THE LOAFER

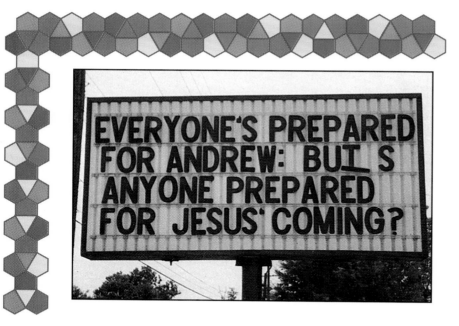

EVERYONE'S PREPARED FOR ANDREW: BUT IS ANYONE PREPARED FOR JESUS' COMING?

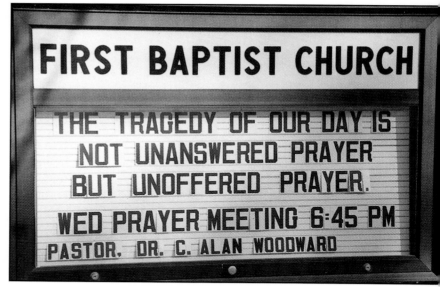

FIRST BAPTIST CHURCH

THE TRAGEDY OF OUR DAY IS NOT UNANSWERED PRAYER BUT UNOFFERED PRAYER.

WED PRAYER MEETING 6:45 PM

PASTOR. DR. C. ALAN WOODWARD

GALILEE BAPTIST CHURCH

PRAY DONT FORGET OR PREY YOU MAY BECOME

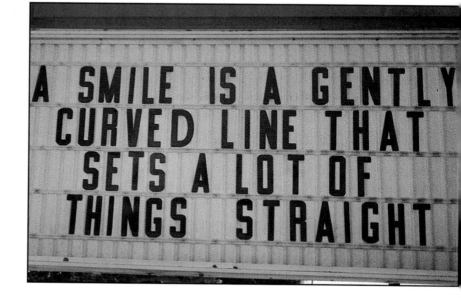

A SMILE IS A GENTLY CURVED LINE THAT SETS A LOT OF THINGS STRAIGHT

ZION BAPTIST CHURCH

YOU ALWAYS HAVE
A FRIEND. WHEN
YOU HAVE GOD WITHIN
REV. KENNETH FARLEY

NO ONE GETS
LOST
ON THE STRAIGHT
ROAD

Gulfcrest Baptist Church
SALVATION IS TODAY
GOD DOES NOT PROMISE
US TOMORROW

AMBASSADOR
BAPTIST CHURCH
SUN. 10 AM
SUN. 6 PM
WED. 7 PM
PASTOR WILLIAM PASCHAL

A CHILD IS MORE LIKELY
TO SEE GOD AS FATHER
IF THEY SEE GOD IN
THEIR FATHER

NEW ERA
MISSIONARY BAPTIST CHURCH

WHEN YOU CAN'T SEE
THE BRIGHT SIDE,
POLISH THE
DULL SIDE.

FIRST BAPTIST CHURCH
PASTOR: GARRY HARRED

A SHARP TONGUE
CAN DULL
A CHRISTIAN'S WITNESS.

Gulfcrest Baptist Church
THE GREATEST SIN OF THIS
AGE IS THE REJECTION OF
JESUS CHRIST

THE
GREATER ANTIOCH
MISSIONARY BAPTIST
CHURCH
DR. JOHN W DAVIS, SR. — PASTOR

THE PERSON
WHO
SERVES,
DESERVES

The Other Side of the Road

Let this be your opportunity to engage in creative thinking. You may want to use this space to record reflections on your faith, family, and friends.

_____

_____

_____

_____

_____

_____

_____

_____

_____

_____

Use this space to paste in photographs of your favorite roadside signs.

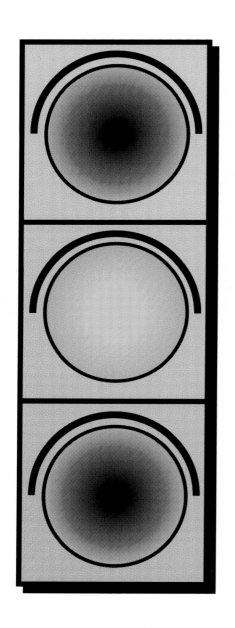

CAUTION

Don't live your life in the middle lane. Keep your eye on the roadside.